D0394225

# I Am
## a Victor

# I Am a Victor

## The **Mordechai Ronen** Story

### MORDECHAI RONEN
With Steve Paikin

*With a Foreword by Canada's
Twentieth Prime Minister, Jean Chrétien*

DUNDURN
TORONTO

Editor: Michael Melgaard
Design: Laura Boyle
Cover design: Avi Dunkelman
Front cover image: *Saba's Smirk* (2011) photomontage by Sari Ronen
Back cover images: courtesy of the Ronen family—(left) Mordechai Ronen with Ronald S. Lauder; (right) Mordechai Ronen with Steven Spielberg
Back flap images: courtesy of the Ronen family
Printer: Friesens

**Library and Archives Canada Cataloguing in Publication**

Ronen, Mordechai, author

I am a victor : the Mordechai Ronen story / Mordechai Ronen ; with Steve Paikin ; foreword by the Right Honourable Jean Chrétien.

Issued in print and electronic formats.
ISBN 978-1-4597-3178-3 (bound).--ISBN 978-1-4597-3179-0 (pdf).-- ISBN 978-1-4597-3180-6 (epub)

1. Ronen, Mordechai. 2. Holocaust survivors--Canada--Biography. 3. Holocaust, Jewish (1939-1945)--Personal narratives. 4. Auschwitz (Concentration camp)--Biography. 5. Jews--Canada--Biography. I. Paikin, Steve, 1960-, author II. Chrétien, Jean, 1934-, writer of preface III. Title.

D804.196.R65 2015                 940.53'18092                 C2015-902075-1
                                                               C2015-902076-X

2   3   4   5     19   18   17   16   15

 Conseil des Arts du Canada    Canada Council for the Arts     Canada     ONTARIO ARTS COUNCIL CONSEIL DES ARTS DE L'ONTARIO an Ontario government agency un organisme du gouvernement de l'Ontario

We acknowledge the support of the **Canada Council for the Arts** and the **Ontario Arts Council** for our publishing program. We also acknowledge the financial support of the **Government of Canada** through the **Canada Book Fund** and **Livres Canada Books**, and the **Government of Ontario** through the **Ontario Book Publishing Tax Credit** and the **Ontario Media Development Corporation**.

Care has been taken to trace the ownership of copyright material used in this book. The author and the publisher welcome any information enabling them to rectify any references or credits in subsequent editions.
— *J. Kirk Howard, President*

The publisher is not responsible for websites or their content unless they are owned by the publisher.

Printed and bound in Canada.

**VISIT US AT**

Dundurn.com | @dundurnpress | Facebook.com/dundurnpress | Pinterest.com/dundurnpress

Dundurn
3 Church Street, Suite 500
Toronto, Ontario, Canada
M5E 1M2

# Contents

# Foreword

Almost five years into my tenure as prime minister of Canada, I decided to make an official state visit to Poland. Growing up as I did in rural Quebec where there was no Jewish community, I was aware of the Holocaust but, frankly, didn't know much about it. It wasn't part of our school curriculum. So this trip presented an opportunity to gain a better understanding of the incredible suffering the Jewish people had experienced in Auschwitz. In fact, the mother of one of my most important policy advisors, Chaviva Hošek, was a survivor of Auschwitz.

So we made the decision that if we were going, we should invite some Canadians who had been to Auschwitz to accompany us. My staff got in touch with the head of the Canadian Jewish Congress, Moshe Ronen, for assistance in arranging a tour, and to invite him to join us.

When I found out that Moshe's father Mordechai was a former prisoner in that concentration camp, I thought it made sense to invite his father to come along with me as well. I later learned that Mordechai Ronen had no intention of accepting my invitation. He had already visited the camp a few years earlier, and found the experience excruciating. Apparently, seeing those gates, the fences, the barracks, the chimneys, even the shoes of those exterminated — well, you could understand how that would overwhelm anyone who had survived that death camp more than half a century earlier.

But I'm happy to say that many people prevailed upon Mordechai to reconsider my offer, and when he did, I insisted that Mordechai travel with me to Auschwitz, in my limousine. As we approached the gates, his emotions understandably got the better of him. He saw those rusty train tracks again, the barbed wire fences, the watch towers, and the sign that proclaimed "Arbeit Macht Frei" (Work Makes You Free). I could see that he was crying and in deep distress. And to be honest, my wife Aline and I had tears in our eyes as well.

Mordechai and I are practically the same age (he's only a year and a half older than I am). So I took his hand in mine and tried to comfort him as best I could. "We'll get through this together, Mordechai," I told him.

And we did.

At one point, I asked him how he was doing in this awful place where members of his own family had been exterminated.

"I came here more than fifty years ago with my family in a cattle car and my parents and sisters were murdered here," he said to me. "Now, I return in the company of my prime minister, in a limousine, with my son who's the head of the Canadian Jewish Community. I feel like a victor!"

Mordechai got out of the limousine, fell to his knees, stretched out his arms and began crying, "I've survived. I'm alive. I'm alive." It was one of the most dramatic and emotional things I had ever seen in my nearly forty years in politics, including nine years in the prime minister's office.

Moshe and I helped lift Mordechai back to his feet, as people around us began hugging him and offering words of comfort. Even journalists joined the crowd, cheering for Mordechai. It was a great moment.

We toured Auschwitz together and said a prayer for all those that had died there. Mordechai couldn't stop the tears from flowing as he looked at me and uttered, "Never again. It must never happen again."

I was the first Canadian prime minister ever to visit Auschwitz. At the time, I described the visit for the reporters covering the trip as "difficult, but necessary."

I always thought you had to be pretty tough to come from a small town in Quebec and climb the greasy pole of politics all the way to the prime minister's office. But that kind of toughness doesn't begin to describe what Mordechai Ronen went through to survive to this day. It was one of the great honours of my time in politics to be able to accompany him to Auschwitz. We can all honour that trip and Mordechai's life by working to ensure that his words to me there have meaning:

"Never again."

The Right Honourable Jean Chrétien
Canada's twentieth Prime Minister

# Introduction

Back in the spring of 1992 I was part of a small delegation made up of journalists, academics, business leaders, and activists from the Canadian Jewish community, who traveled to Poland with a particular purpose.

My job was simple: observe and consider whether what I saw could be the makings of a future documentary I might produce for TVO, Ontario's provincial public broadcaster. However, for other members of the delegation, the mission was more delicate and critical. Those members were tasked with determining whether Poland had made enough progress in combatting anti-Semitism, to the point where the group could recommend that Canadians Jews travel to Poland the following year.

It was an important question because the following year — April 19, 1993, to be exact — was the fiftieth anniversary of the Warsaw Ghetto Uprising, one of the most significant events in the history of the Jewish people. The uprising marked the first real, orchestrated attempt by Jews to fight their extermination at the hands of the Nazis. When the word got out that this brave group of ghetto residents, hopelessly outgunned and outnumbered as they were, tried to fight back against efforts to liquidate them, it gave enormous hope to fearful and victimized Jews worldwide.

Officials in the Canadian Jewish community surmised that there could be significant interest among a large number of Canadian Jews of Polish descent to return to the land of their birth to observe the pending anniversary. But first, this small delegation needed to determine whether those Jews would be welcomed.

One of the members of that delegation was Mordechai Ronen. Mordechai, sixty-one years old at the time, made what must have been an excruciating decision: to return to the scene of the most monstrous crime in world history, and confront his part in it. With his thirty-four-year-old son Moshe, he visited the Auschwitz concentration camp, where he had been taken and imprisoned as a child of eleven. On the bus on the way to Auschwitz, I started asking Mordechai questions about those times. His son Moshe watched and listened silently. Through the course of our conversation, Moshe heard his father reveal deeply personal details about the Holocaust he had never before heard. For example, Mordechai referred to his father, mother, and two sisters, one of whom was pregnant, who were taken to Auschwitz and never seen again. Until that moment, Moshe had never known that he had two aunts. His father had never spoken of them before. For Mordechai, the memory of losing his parents and two siblings to the Holocaust had always been too painful to discuss with his family. That was the case for so many of his generation.

Eventually, we arrived at Auschwitz, and saw the gates that famously and cynically offered up the false promise that work would make the prisoners free.

To say the day was filled with extraordinarily emotional moments doesn't begin to describe what transpired. At one moment, Mordechai found himself standing beside the crematoria in the adjoining Birkenau death camp, where more than a million Jews, Romani, prostitutes, mentally ill, homosexuals, and other "undesirables" had their ashes go up the smoke stacks. He looked up to the heavens and shouted to the spirit of his deceased father: "*Tateh!* Look! Look what I have brought here!" Then pointing to his son Moshe (who was named after his father), he continued, "I have brought back a living monument of our family." We were all sobbing uncontrollably at Mordechai's message of triumph. Hitler, he seemed to be saying, you may have killed much of my family. But I'm still here. And there's another generation behind me.

Our group finished its ten-day mission. We met with many senior Polish government officials and some representatives of the small but hardy Polish Jewish community, which once numbered more than three million, but now numbers less than ten thousand. Our group determined that Poland did feel different, that it was, in fact, ready to welcome thousands of Jewish tourists for the fiftieth anniversary of the Warsaw Ghetto Uprising. The following year, almost 150 Jews from Canada visited Warsaw. I returned as well to follow the exploits of three families, the parents of whom were Warsaw Ghetto survivors, who were showing their children (in some cases for the first time) where they lived and how they survived such madness. The documentary was called *Return to the Warsaw Ghetto*, and still airs on TVO from time to time.

The Ronens and Paikins had been family friends for more than a decade. But our experience in Poland in 1992 connected us as never before. And so, when Mordechai Ronen determined that the time had come for him to tell the story of how he survived the Holocaust, not just to a few of us on a bus but, rather, to the whole world, his family chose me to tell that story. I shall be forever grateful that they did.

As you make your way through this book, I suspect you'll share my astonishment at the moments and events that Mordechai has managed to confront and survive. In some respects, he was like feather buffeted through the air, finding himself in extraordinarily dangerous circumstances, almost none of which were of his choosing. There was a randomness to the evil he was regularly forced to confront. And yet, at almost every turn, whether he understood it or not, Mordechai was required to make a decision — a choice — that could either save his life for another day, or result in his death. There were so many others who could not endure the daily agony of the Holocaust. Understandably, many actively chose suicide or simply gave up the desire to live. And none of us can judge them.

But Mordechai chose life. Even when his world turned completely upside down, he always chose life.

Mordechai Ronen's story may not be unique. But it is his story. And the world should consider itself lucky, as I write this, that he is still around to tell it.

Steve Paikin

Toronto, Ontario

September, 2015

# 1

# Paradise Lost

If you're reading this book and you were born in a place such as Canada or the United States, my first revelation here is going to seem a little strange, because if you ask a Canadian or an American what country they were born in, the answer is pretty obvious.

Not so with me.

You have to understand the way the world worked eighty-three years ago when I was born. Borders of countries changed all the time, because of wars or deals made by the great powers. So I was born on June 5, 1932, in a little town called Dej (pronounced with a soft J, sort of like Dezh). In fact, it's still there today, nestled in to the Romanian countryside. Dej was a typical eastern European town — small, insignificant, just like hundreds of others that dotted the European landscape in the first half of the twentieth century. Legend has it that nomadic tribes stopped there to rest and cried out three times in Latin: Deus, the word for God. And so the town got its name that way. Its population today is about thirty thousand, but it was only half that when I lived there, and was made up mostly of Transylvanians, Hungarians, Roma, and yes, a pretty sizeable Jewish community as well.

For me, Dej was a paradise. It was home. But my little part of the world had been caught up in some severe political undercurrents after the First World War. It had been the capital of Szolnok-Doboka County in Hungary from 1918 through 1920. But then, thanks to the Treaty of Trianon in 1920, Dej was handed over to Romania. Actually, because of Dej's location, it had changed hands many times throughout history. The Austrians, the Hungarians, even the Ottomans all once ruled over it. About a year after the Second World War started, my little town changed countries again. Through the Vienna Awards, Germany and Italy compelled Romania to cede half of Dej's region (Transylvania) to Hungary on August 30, 1940. So once again, Dej was back in Hungarian hands. This generated a lot of migration among some populations, but frankly, didn't change our lives at all. (After the Second World War, the Paris Peace Treaties returned our region to Romania yet again).

In hindsight, I should have been prouder to live in northern Transylvania, with its exotic legend of Count Dracula, the fifteenth century Transylvanian prince believed to have lived in the region and who drank the blood of unsuspecting maidens with his vampire-bat-like fangs. I'm sorry to disappoint you, but even though I lived in Transylvania, I never saw any evidence of the count!

Back then, I also had a different name. I was born Mordechai Shlomo Markovits, although I did get called by a couple of different nicknames. Modche Shloymeh was one. It's basically the same as my real name, with just a more Yiddish-sounding pronunciation. My brothers and some cousins used to call me Kitchee, which basically means "Little Hungarian."

You might find it strange, but we really didn't care that our country had changed from Hungarian to Romanian hands and back. Our ethnic identification centred more on our Jewish faith, rather than any particular country we lived in. I still went to the same school. My father still went to work and served the same customers. My mother still kept house for her five children, of which I was the youngest. Really, the only thing that seemed to change was the flag.

The Jewish community in Dej actually constituted about 20 percent of the town's population. And we had quite a long history there. Officially, Jews were banned from settling in Dej until 1848, but the prohibition must not have been very strictly enforced. As early as 1805 there were seventy Jewish residents there. Once the ban was officially lifted, more Jewish families from Galicia (the border region between present day Ukraine and Poland) began moving to Dej. They were overwhelmingly Orthodox with a strong Chassidic element.

They began to establish Jewish institutions in the town, such as the first *shul* (synagogue) built in 1863, then another in 1907. That second synagogue was particularly dear to me, since it was built just a few steps from our home. I really considered it my home away from home — that's how much of our life was centred on that *shul*. It was just a gorgeous building with beautiful decorations inside and out, exquisite patchworks in the windows, and many ancient books and sacraments on the shelves.

Our Jewish community in Dej began to grow. More synagogues were opened to serve other sects of Judaism (I think there were seven or eight in all); social halls and yeshivas (Jewish seminaries) followed. We were all a pretty multilingual bunch. We spoke Yiddish inside the community, and either Hungarian or Romanian to the ethnic majority around us.

We had a brick house, painted white, that looked like any other in the neighbourhood. It was on Kodur Street. It wasn't very big, but seemed big enough for my two older brothers, two older sisters, and me. There was a garden in the backyard. We grew plums, peaches, cherries, and apples, which became staples of our diet. I can still smell the wonderful aroma of my mother's delicious goulash, or the scent of Shabbat candles, the sounds of Shabbat prayers, and the laughter and chatter of my sisters. With only five kids, ours was a relatively small family. We saw other Jewish families with a dozen kids.

Let me tell you a bit about my father, whose name was Moshe, after whom my first son is named. He was the son of Tzvi and Yenta Markovits, and I always called him *tateh*, the Yiddish word for father. Sadly, there are no documents that can prove what I'm about to say, but I'm relatively certain that my father was born around 1895 in one of the smaller villages near Dej. Like so many other Jewish men of the time, he was a merchant — a travelling salesman — who went from one town to another, by train, by horse and buggy, even on foot to sell food, clothes, medicines, or kitchenware. Our predominantly rural region didn't have much industry, but textile mills — cloth and fabric production — were one of the few developed businesses. My father would buy his merchandise from the factories, then sell those rolls of cloth, belts, gloves, and even ties to his customers. And there was more. My father would also buy products from local farmers then sell them in Dej. He worked hard. Oftentimes, he disappeared for a week when he went on the road. But he always made a special effort to be home for Shabbat and he never went on long road trips before important Jewish holidays. When he came home, we'd always have a bit of a celebration to welcome him back.

My mother was born Elka Harnik, the daughter of Abraham and Tova Harnik, and I have to confess, I'm somewhat confused as to where she and her family originally come from. I always thought my mother was born in Vienna, today the capital of Austria, but which was then the capital of the Austro-Hungarian Empire. Of course she spoke Yiddish, but she also spoke excellent German, which supports my belief. But other records suggest she was born in a place called Nasaud, in the historical region of Transylvania in northern Romania. It could be that her parents were from Vienna and moved to Romania, which would also explain why she spoke German so well.

My mother's origins were actually the subject of a conversation with a previous attorney-general of Ontario. In the late 1990s when Mike Harris was premier of Ontario, he and my son Moshe struck up a friendship, having frequently met through their respective political activities. One evening, Moshe had me, the premier, and Ontario's attorney-general over to his home for dinner. The attorney-general's name was Charles Harnick, the

MPP for Willowdale. Harnick pointed out his ancestors were also from Austria, and when we noted the similarity between his last name and my mother's, we had a good laugh speculating as to whether we were all related.

In any event, I do know my mother moved to Dej at the age of eighteen or nineteen, for a very specific reason: to marry my father! I'm still vague on many of the details surrounding my parents' marriage. It's quite possible theirs was an "arranged marriage," meaning their two families had set it up on the grounds of their shared religious tradition. (Remember the matchmaker in *Fiddler on the Roof?* Something like that.)

My mother always followed the strict traditions of Orthodox Judaism. For example, she always wore a *sheitel* (a wig) because, in the interests of modesty, married Jewish women were expected to cover their heads. I don't know if she had any aspirations or dreams beyond being a good wife to my father, taking care of the house, and attending to the needs of her children. Expectations were obviously quite different in those days. Women in eastern European towns didn't have the choice of being wives and mothers, or career girls. Although, as I look back, I recall my mother constantly being in motion. She was always doing something. Hers was more than a full-time job. Almost every piece of clothing we five kids had, she made. Only heavier coats and shoes would be purchased. She was an artistic, creative soul who loved culture, but certainly never had the time to engage in it seriously. But I do remember a book always being within reach of my mother's grasp, and if she had a moment to herself, she would read a page or two.

She also wrote songs in Yiddish and Hungarian. I thought she had a real gift for music and poetry. She would sit on the edge of my bed at night and read to me, or sing her own songs to help me fall asleep. Her voice was rich and tender, and conveyed deep emotion and feeling. My favourite lullaby was called "Ilulu." It was a Yiddish song that she sang to me as she rocked me to sleep. "Hilu, lulu, schaefeleh schluf mein teir kind" (the "Hilu, lulu" are just cooing sounds — they don't really mean anything. But the rest of the line roughly translates to "Sleep well, my precious little child"). I was probably two or three years old when she did this.

I also learned a skill from my mother that no one else in the family had: the ability to speak German. At home, we spoke mostly Yiddish and Hungarian, but with my mom, the occasional bit of German too. Because it sounded so much like Yiddish, it was easy to pick up. (Yiddish is a language whose roots are in the small towns of ninth-century central Europe. It sounds German but is written with the Hebrew alphabet.) Little did I know that those German lessons from my mother would prove to be most helpful later in life, albeit under tragic circumstances.

Let me tell you about my siblings. My oldest sister was named Tobi, whom I think was born around 1922. One of my strongest memories of her was her wedding day, because we got to take a bus to attend the wedding. That was unusual. Again, I suspect there was some family matchmaking at play for the couple. Tobi's husband's name was Chaim Itzhak (I can't remember his last name), and he was a very religious yeshiva student. I only met him for the first time at the wedding. After the wedding, Tobi moved out to live with Chaim Itzhak and he got a job teaching at a Jewish school. We saw much less of the couple after that — maybe Friday night Shabbat dinners at our home. But we would be reunited under tragic circumstances later in life.

My other sister's name was Sara, but we always called her Suri — it seems everyone in the family had a nickname. Suri was only a couple of years older than me, having been born in 1930, and was hugely important to me in my early years. She was the sibling I spent the most time with. With my mother always busy, my father always on the road, and my older brothers off at yeshiva, Suri was the one who was sort of "in charge" of me. She kept me engaged, entertained, and safe. She was my best childhood friend. And yet, to this day, I have difficulty remembering more about her: what she looked like, what her voice sounded like, the funny things that we did together — these things have faded from my memory and I don't know why.

Could it be that the truth of what happened to my dear Suri was so awful, my mind is protecting me from the torture that would surely persist if I were to remember more? How is it possible that I can't even remember what she looked like? And, of course, no pictures have survived those times.

Besides my two older sisters, I had two older brothers as well. David was the second oldest child after Tobi, and yes, we had a nickname for him too: Dudi. He was ten years older than me. My other brother was Shalom, we called him Shuli, and he was seven years my senior. They had both left to study at a yeshiva by the time I was nine years old. Strangely enough, there were yeshivas in Dej, but my father chose to send them to a yeshiva that was further away from home. Perhaps he thought this would hasten their independence and better prepare them for the real life complexities that were just around the corner. In hindsight, it was a remarkably prescient decision. While I did miss my brothers, the bright side was more time and space for Suri and me.

I didn't see much of my maternal grandparents, given that they lived in Vienna. And after a time, I didn't see much of my paternal grandparents either. They lived just outside Dej, but they were old and frail and couldn't come to our house much. We tended to see them at their home, for example for Passover Seder, when the whole family would get together. Those were wonderful times — everyone smiling, laughing, and happy to be in each other's company. We actually had a very large family in and around Dej, believe it or not, up to two hundred cousins, aunts, and uncles. But once again, for some reason, only a half dozen or so are still in my mind. Even my grandparents' names escape me, although we recently found some documentation that shed some light on their identities. The only time we were all truly together was when the authorities established a Jewish ghetto, essentially imprisoning us all there. But I'm getting ahead of myself. That story is still to come.

So I hope you're getting a better sense of what life was like in Dej. Everybody seemed to know everybody on our mostly Jewish street. We frequently got together with the neighbours; they were as welcomed in our home as we were in theirs. At holiday time, we'd cook for each other. It just felt like one big, extended family.

Today, the prime custom seems to consist of people getting together for backyard barbeques. Not so back then. The synagogue was the centre of communal life, and our synagogue was just a few steps away from our home. Given that my father was a particularly religious man, we had all the more reason to immerse ourselves in *shul* life. All of the synagogues in Dej

accommodated the various branches of Judaism, from orthodox to reform. Our *shul* was orthodox, but not ultra-orthodox
or Chassidic. My father did wear a beard but he was not a
huge stickler for the outward manifestations of our faith. In
other words, he didn't wear *payot* (the ringlets of hair on each
side of his head traditionally worn by ultra-Orthodox Jews),
nor did he wear his *tzitzit* (the four-cornered ritual garment
with a series of strings and knots on each corner) on the outside of his clothing. More important to him was the essence
of Judaism — a love for God, and a respect for our fellow citizens. I can still remember him explaining that to all of us kids.

The synagogue was my second home. If my mother ever
wondered where I was after school, she knew exactly where I'd
be. From the time I was three years old, that *shul* was a huge
part of my life. I can recall my father taking me there at age
three for an important Jewish rite of passage: the *upsherin*, my
first haircut. I suspect this ceremony is no longer practised
by most Jews today, but the custom is alive and well in the
Orthodox Jewish world. And among Orthodox Jews in eastern Europe, it certainly was a big deal. The extended family
would gather after the haircutting for a special celebration. My
father wrapped me in his *tallit* (prayer shawl). This may be the
earliest recollection in my life that stays with me. I still clearly
see in my mind's eye the memory of my father, so young and
strong, moved by the importance of the moment.

After the *upsherin*, a Jewish boy's life is supposed to get
more serious. Yes, at age three! Primarily, that meant going
to a Jewish parochial school, learning more about the faith,
and for me, joining the synagogue choir. My confidence got a

boost during these early years. My father had taught me how to sing well, and his lessons must have helped since I got a solo part during one of the High Holiday services. I became a bit of a "child star" in the Jewish community. Whether it was Hanukkah or some other holiday, little Motke always seemed to have a featured role in the performance. In fact, that was often the case with most members of my family. Of course, we did have a cantor at the *shul*, but everyone in the Markovits family seemed to pitch in: my father brought his great sense of rhythm and tone; my mother and two sisters were always ready to sing along; and Dudi and Shuli were exceptional performers. Singing brought me so much joy, and I did it every day of my life until I was eleven, when the singing all stopped for reasons I will soon describe.

Daily routine was very important to our family and of course it revolved around the synagogue. In the morning, we went to *shul* before school, and also again in the evening. (You can see the word *shul* closely resembles the word school, which is no coincidence — the *shul* was a place of constant learning.)

As I got a little older, I started going to two schools: a public school, with its government-approved curriculum, for a few hours during the day; then *chayder*, an after-school program for Jewish studies. And there was praying — lots of praying — in the morning, afternoon, and evening, all religious routines a good Jewish boy was required to follow. There was little time for leisure; our schedules were too busy. In fact, the only time I can recall being outside to play with other kids was on school holidays, where we might indulge in a game of hide-and-seek with the boys who lived next door. We also played with sheep bones. Yes, you read that correctly. What can I say? We didn't have too many toys.

If you're a young person reading this, who perhaps goes to a school with kids from all over the world, this will also seem strange: all the kids in my day basically stuck to their own kind. The Jewish kids and Christian kids might have said "hello" and "goodbye" to each other during the course of the day, but not much more. I never thought of it as bad blood or prejudice. We simply lived in different areas with different traditions. As a kid, I never felt any overt anti-Semitism around me, although there were times when my parents warned me not to stay out too late when night fell early, lest some Christian kids "who might not like your side-locks would pick on you." I always interpreted that as just having overprotective parents.

So we all took joy in our daily routines and expected life to continue that way, with one exception. My father often talked about immigrating to Israel someday. He was a strong Zionist, devout in his faith, and he believed Israel was the Holy Land and home for all Jews.

But until that day came, we would make the best of living in Dej, and that meant something my father often told us: "If somebody stretches out a hand, you should always give." We followed his example. On holidays, we filled bags with presents and food for those who had less than we did. On Mondays and Thursdays we typically had somebody over to our home to share in our dinner. We weren't special in that. My recollection is, everyone did it. For example, one time my mother got quite sick to the point where seeing a doctor became necessary. Remember: we had no Medicare in Dej. So going to the doctor was a big decision. I can recall at the time, my father was going through a rough patch with his business, and we really didn't have money for doctors. But my mother saw the doctor anyway, promising to pay some time down the road when our economic circumstances improved. To the doctor, that was perfectly fine. That's how it worked back then. People trusted each other, regardless of religion or ethnicity. (And the doctor in question wasn't Jewish.)

So that was Dej in the 1930s and early 1940s. We thought it would always be this way.

Turned out, we were wrong.

# 2

# A Gathering Storm

I lived in a home with no daily newspaper, no radio, and no telephone. Of course, television hadn't been invented yet. So the only way we could keep up to date on how the Second World War was proceeding was at *shul.* You'd hear snippets of conversations among the adults. Essentially, our life in Dej remained the same and there just wasn't much talk at the dinner table about such matters.

But as the war raged on, we did begin to notice a change in our otherwise tranquil life, starting toward the end of 1942 or beginning of 1943. Suddenly, we Jews in Dej saw evidence of anger toward us. Before long, our Hungarian neighbours became more audacious and insulting in their contempt for us. How did the sunny skies suddenly turn so cloudy? Trips to and from school became dangerous. I hadn't changed. I was still the same nice and friendly person I'd always been. But the others, who'd been equally as friendly before, were now hurling stones and racial epithets at us.

"Zsidók, menjetek ki! Gyerünk haza! A Palesztin! Ez nem az otthoni itt!" they'd shout in Hungarian (Jews, get out of here! Go home! Go to your Palestine! It's not your home here!). I complained to my father, but what could he do?

I recall one time, while our synagogue choir was rehearsing, the sound of broken glass interrupted our singing. A rock had shattered our beautiful stained-glass window. The adults told us not to move as they went outside to check what had happened. But the street was dark and empty. The rabbi tried to convince us this was likely the work of a lone, drunken troublemaker, and not to take it seriously. Even though I was a child of ten, I knew better.

With no access to media, we relied on new arrivals to Dej to keep up with the news from elsewhere in Europe. One time, I noticed four or five new men in our synagogue, who had just escaped from Poland, no doubt with forged passports and the like. They shocked us with stories we found impossible to believe. They claimed that in Poland, Nazis were rounding up Jews from their homes, looting their possessions, and then murdering them. No normal person would believe such things. People said they were *meshuggah* (crazy). These Jewish Poles insisted the same fate would befall all of us. One man told us about Lodz, his hometown, which before the war had one of the biggest Jewish communities in Europe, with a population of two hundred thousand. Now, he claimed, Lodz was devoid of Jews. They had all been rounded up, taken to concentration camps, and killed.

How could it be, we wondered? Wouldn't it be physically impossible to exterminate thousands upon thousands of innocent, law-abiding people? No, people concluded, this just wasn't possible. We were certain that fear had prompted these Polish émigrés to exaggerate.

There were other factors at play as well. Some of the Poles spoke little if any Yiddish, and we didn't speak Polish. So communication was a problem. And, of course, there was no mass media in Dej allowing independent verification of these wild stories. The authorities had confiscated the few radio sets some residents in Dej might have had, lest the people fall prey to disinformation spread by the enemy. Telephones were a rarity as well. Only government offices had them. I seem to recall one person declined to turn in his short wave radio, and secretly listened to the British Broadcasting Corporation newscasts. He then told a few sources what he had heard. But it also seemed to have little impact on the community. We knew Hungary was part of the German war Axis. But that all felt very far away. We all assumed the hardships of poorly stocked shelves in supermarkets was temporary, that things would eventually improve, and go back to normal. After all, Christians and Jews had lived together relatively peacefully in Hungary for centuries. Why should everything change, just because the Nazis had taken over Germany? Berlin was almost 1,400 kilometres northwest of Dej. Today, that's an airplane ride of a little more than two hours. Seven decades ago, we thought of distances that large as being in another solar system. None of that should have affected us, we thought.

It was very wishful thinking. And so, we took no particular precautions against the looming storm. Even our wise rabbi at the *shul* simply said of the Poles, let them speak. Maybe he thought letting them pour out their hearts from the *bimah* (the podium or stage at the front of the synagogue) would be somehow cathartic for our Polish visitors. But no one took their admonitions seriously. Yes, perhaps their relatives had been taken away by the Nazi authorities, and maybe no one had seen them in a year. But surely that didn't mean they were all dead? The absence of any proof allowed us to continue to live in our fantasy world that everything would work itself out in the end.

Still, some members of our community did consider, what if? What if they're telling the truth? What if the Nazis had designs on the Jewish community in Hungary? Could we avoid a similar fate? We had heard other stories about Jews leaving the cities of other German-occupied places and hiding in the forests. But that wasn't an option in Dej. The forests just weren't thick enough to hide in. The Hungarian gendarmerie could easily find stragglers hiding in the woods. So that option was ultimately rejected.

I heard others discuss the possibility of getting forged documents, and taking on new (non-Jewish) identities. But we figured that would only work in the most remote parts of the country where the authorities were unlikely to show up. But even then, you would have to depend on potentially unfriendly neighbours and not raise their suspicions. As we would come to learn, not many would risk their lives to save strange Jews; most would rather sell them out to ingratiate themselves with the authorities. Only a lucky few were able to hide in plain sight and avoid catastrophe. But the only impact these stories seemed to have on my family was a cache of extra potatoes and bread that I discovered stashed away in our basement — a minor precautionary measure taken by my mother.

By 1943 the messages became more frequent and more reliable. Strangers from Budapest and Warsaw warned us to prepare for pending danger. My father stopped travelling to some towns because the local people had clearly hardened their attitudes towards doing business with Jews. "Jó reggelt, Mr. Markovitz" (Good morning Mr. Markovits), was replaced with "A zsidó szakálla, menj vissza a Palesztin" (Jew with the beard, go back to your Palestine). One day, my father came home clean-shaven. Some people had grabbed him, held him down, and cut his beard. I stopped going to public school because the non-Jewish kids were now regularly attacking us, and uttering the same threats: "Menj vissza a Palesztinába!" (Go back to your Palestine!). They would mock us with a sense of superiority. We felt vulnerable and humiliated. Even attending *chayder* wasn't safe. My parents, at first, gave me a lantern to carry when I walked home after dark. But eventually, I was no longer permitted to leave by myself; I had to wait for my mother to pick me up and bring me home.

Did the Hungarians I'd lived with my whole life really hate us Jews? I wanted to think not. I wanted to think a cruel minority simply overtook the majority, making everyone irrational.

There were exceptions. There was a cleaning lady who seemed to sympathize with us and did us the odd favour. She also tried to convince us that no one would take us to a concentration camp, that at worst, we'd be taken to a labour camp to await the war's end. The woman was Romanian, like the Jews, another minority in our city. She didn't much like Hungarians either. We appreciated her support.

Stories had got back to Dej that Germany was losing the war and this nightmare might soon end. However, one day, I was clearly disabused of that notion. The Hungarian gendarmes came to our house and ransacked it. They took all our precious possessions including a big Shabbat candelabra.

No, the war wasn't coming to an end. In fact, things were about to get much, much worse.

# 3

# The Ghetto

The news coming back from elsewhere in Europe was predictably scarce, but at the same time, we thought it encouraging. We heard that the Germans had suffered enormous losses during the six-month-long Battle of Stalingrad, which ended in February 1943. It felt as if the tide was turning for the Allied powers, and that the war was coming to an end. Germany's allies in Hungary felt it too, and were looking for ways to make a deal with the Soviet Union. The Nazis didn't take kindly to that and so they invaded Hungary in March 1944, installing a puppet government more aligned to Germany's wishes in the process.

The Nazis ordered all Jews living outside Budapest to be rounded up and placed in ghettos. Given the size of our community, this order required several "operations" to carry out. We got word of the first sweep taking place in the first week of

May 1944. The Jews were to report to the Bungur Forest, where a ghetto was established behind barbed wire. Then we heard reports of a second sweep.

Then it was our turn. And that was the day our misery truly began. Hungarian soldiers simply entered our homes without knocking and told us we had half an hour to pack whatever things we could fit into a suitcase, that we were leaving our homes and would be taken elsewhere. We didn't need half an hour. We knew the drill and within minutes were prepared to leave. I wore my "custom-made" shoes, which a local shoemaker and family friend had made for me. These shoes had a special hiding place for money. We wrongly assumed this craziness would be over quickly, and that whatever money I could hide and take with me would help restart our lives soon.

As we left the house, we saw our little street teeming with Jewish families, standing in a line with their suitcases. I spotted a non-Jewish woman who had been a long-time family friend. She lived across the road from us, often dropping by for a chat with my mother. Sometimes, we hired her to help with meals if we had several people coming over for dinner. She was always paid for her trouble. But her days of friendship had come to an end. She apparently knew everyone's home well and told the authorities where everyone's valuables were hidden. My father had a secret stash; his friend, a painter, had helped him make a hole in the wall inside our house, and then painted it over so that nobody would notice any traces of recent work. My father told us where that "rainy day" stash was hidden. The Hungarian gendarmes walked directly toward it and without hesitating for an instant, broke the wall and took all our money. Our "friend" across the road had turned on us. Apparently, she was even shrewder than that. Yes, she told the authorities where many families kept their secret stashes. But she didn't tell them everything, and when the houses were emptied, she apparently went back and helped herself to more. She announced triumphantly: "Now I will get it all! I will get everything that you have!" She wanted everyone to know how smart she was and for us to acknowledge that. I will never forget her.

We discovered that for the next two weeks, we would be part of contingent of 7,500 Jews corralled into a makeshift ghetto, after which we were to be transported to labour camps. Where? Again, we didn't know.

There was also a symbolic change that would accompany our material change. Henceforth, the Jews of Dej were all to wear yellow Stars of David, further identifying and separating us from the rest of the populace. We were to be stigmatized as the evil within an otherwise peaceful community. Did those yellow stars feel like targets on our chests and backs? They certainly did.

We didn't know it at the time, but we were about to experience the worst the Holocaust had to offer. The madness was just beginning. I've often wondered whether the Nazis could have committed their atrocities with such "success" had their non-German allies not so willingly assisted them. What if the local gendarmeries or residents had refused to co-operate? How might that have stymied the Nazis' plans? How many more families might have survived? There was presumably no way for the Nazis to know everyone who was Jewish. They depended on the willing conspiracy of their neighbouring anti-Semites to round up, escort, guard, transport, and eventually murder their local Jews. The Germans couldn't have done it by themselves. Why did they have so many willing accomplices?

In Dej, our Hungarian neighbours prepared the horses and carts that were waiting to transport us to the ghetto. Only the sick and elderly were allowed to sit on those carts. All others had to walk with their possessions in hand. We were informed that we were being taken to the Bungur Forest to await our fate. What we weren't informed of was that this was the day the Jewish community in Dej died. Few of us would survive. And of those of us who did, maybe one thousand returned, but almost none stayed. Almost a century and a half of Jewish presence in Dej was coming to an end.

It took us several hours to walk the four or five kilometres to our newly built ghetto in the forest. The old, infirm, and very young kept the procession slow. I suspect something else contributed to the slow pace of things. We were all terrified of arriving at our destination and what that might portend. That sick feeling we all had in the pits of our stomachs was the fear that we should have listened more carefully to the warnings offered by our Polish émigrés. We were told that good jobs in a labour camp awaited us. But few among us believed those promises.

We finally arrived at the ghetto and settled in for the first night. As odd as this sounds, it was actually located in a beautiful place. For many years, people came to this forest, climbed on a small hillcrest to enjoy the town's picturesque and splendid views. It was a favorite picnic area where Dej residents used to gather on the first warm days of spring. And since it was now spring, some of the trees were already in blossom. In that respect, we were lucky. We slept outdoors in our clothes. There were no tents. Thankfully, the weather was warming up.

Apparently, the conditions were too luxurious for some local Hungarians, who thought we were being too fairly accommodated. There was a contributor to the weekly newspaper in Dej called *Szamos Volgye* (in English it translates to Somes Valley). His name was Sztojka Laszlo. Laszlo regretted that the Jewish ghetto was established in the Bungur Forest. "It is too beautiful of a place for the Jews. They should have been taken to the open fields to acquaint themselves with nature." He was criticizing the authorities for being too humane with us.

He needn't have worried too much. The ghetto was merely a way station for the torment that was to come. It was our community's temporary residence before being transported elsewhere; to what, we didn't know.

Ironically, this ghetto provided my extended family with our final opportunity to be together. Our family "reunion" consisted of many relatives from both my mother's and father's side. Both my sisters were with us, including Tobi, who was now a few months pregnant. However, my older brothers were not there. Remember, they had been sent out of town by my father since their early teenage years to study at the yeshiva. We had no idea where they were or what their fate might be. All we knew was, they weren't with us behind the barbed wire, confined to the ghetto in Dej.

People did their best to try to make this place home. They stretched blankets over tree branches to create makeshift tents in which to sleep. We gathered branches to make a fire to cook our meals. Each family took care of its own needs. There was a small ration for each, usually beans, potatoes, and a piece of bread. Meat was never on the menu. I got into the habit of stashing away a little piece of my bread for later. Then, at bedtime, I would treat myself to what seemed like the sweetest candy I'd ever tasted.

There was no water in this ghetto. It had to be delivered by fire trucks. People stood in long lines with pitchers and buckets to have something to drink. They were slowly starving and dehydrating us, although we kids were a little less worse off than the adults, who often sacrificed some of their own portions to keep their children's bellies more satiated.

There is sometimes something about the human spirit that is truly remarkable in these circumstances. Some of the non-Jews reacted to this depravity with tremendous decency and generosity. One day, a Moldavian man — I think his name was Mihai — brought his cow to the ghetto. He had heard that the Jews were starving and decided to help. He was arrested and beaten to a pulp. He remained a paraplegic for the rest of his life. The gendarmes needed to set an example — Jews were not to be helped.

Another time a German officer approached us, searching for a specific inmate whose name was Jakab Singer. The officer lived in the house that had belonged to Singer. He arrived with soldiers and a car loaded with food for the Jews. The soldiers that were accompanying him unloaded flour, sugar, rice, lard, beans, compotes, and pickles from the trunk. Astonishing.

For most people, the ghetto was a prison camp. They remained inside the wire until it was time to be transported elsewhere. But for me, it was a different story. Being young and small, the Hungarian guards occasionally let me leave the ghetto to find food elsewhere in town. Presumably they assumed

I wouldn't run off without my parents and they were right. I always returned. My mother would give me some money or items to exchange, and so I would go to the next town or village and bring back some additional bread or potatoes. I tried to get more information out of my parents about what was happening. I always had the sense they were holding back things from me. My questions were almost always answered with, "Don't you worry; everything will be fine."

Before long, the Dej ghetto was becoming filthy. Obviously, we had no bathroom facilities. We weren't able to wash our clothes. There was no medical help or medicine for the sick. Diseases started spreading; some of the old and sick died. The bodies were removed and buried outside the camp. As if this weren't bad enough, there were also murders in our ghetto. The guards had no patience with some inmates and any confrontation could end in death. After the war, some of the survivors exhumed the bodies from the forest and reburied them in the local Jewish cemetery.

Eventually, the situation in the ghetto improved a little when the authorities agreed to expand the territory of the encampment to incorporate a small brook at the bottom of the forest. At least then the people could wash themselves, their clothes, and their dishes. The new expanded territory even included some sort of emergency hospital with a staff of physicians, although still with almost no medicines. Some of what they had to deal with was too horrific for two of the doctors in the ghetto. Documents and memoirs have reported the names of two doctors who tried to commit suicide on the eve of the first deportation transport. Doctor Szocs, a middle-aged man from Debrecen (the second largest city in Hungary after Budapest), and Dr. Biro, a young man from Budapest, injected each other with morphine, and also swallowed a lethal dose of the drug. The older man agonized for twenty-four hours, while constantly calling out for his children in a delirious state. The younger man with a stronger constitution somehow survived. They must have known what was going to happen to them and their patients.

The ghetto administration told us we would be taken to labour camps in several groups, according to our age. Children, we were told, wouldn't be worked too hard, and would be assigned something commensurate with their abilities. Rumours abounded. From time to time, we would hear that we would be transported not on a regular passenger train, but rather in cattle cars. I would overhear the leaders of the Jewish community in the ghetto discussing these kinds of things. There actually was a sort of Jewish administration responsible for keeping us under control and informed, mostly about when food would be distributed. I wouldn't say these people were akin to the infamous *kapos* who collaborated with the Nazis in concentration camps. They were respected members of our community: rabbis, synagogue presidents, school administrators, etc.

Remarkably, the security around the ghetto was by no means airtight. Some people successfully escaped. Among them was one member of the Panet family from Dej — a dynasty of local rabbis who had served in the city for almost one hundred years. He eventually found shelter in Romania. Later, he moved to Israel where he continued the dynasty working as a rabbi.

People often discussed the possibility of escaping. Few actually attempted it. It was dangerous. You had to assume if you were caught, you'd be killed. And besides, people didn't want to abandon their wives and children. Who knows what retribution would be meted out on those left behind? Beyond that, how would one find food and shelter, or evade the local police who would undoubtedly send out search parties? How long before one of the locals would see an escapee and turn them in? When people ask, why didn't you try to escape, why didn't you put up more of a fight? My answer is, it's easy to say that in the comfort of today's world. But you have to understand: we were hungry, tired, terrified, vulnerable, and constantly hoping the war would end, bringing this madness to a conclusion. While things were bad, something inside us just refused to believe that things could get even worse.

Of course, they could and would get much worse.

My father considered an escape attempt. Before doing so, he talked to the rabbi from our synagogue, who discouraged him from doing so. The rabbi told him he would be much safer in a labour camp, rather than hiding in the woods and endangering those he would leave behind.

"We just have to accept our fate here," the rabbi told him. "What will happen to you will happen to all of us."

My father abandoned his plans. Still, it's hard to know how we could have done it anyway. I was only twelve years old, one of my sisters was pregnant, and our physical condition was already much degraded. We simply wanted to believe that there was an easier way to get through this predicament. And even if we were transported to a labour camp, why would the Germans want to destroy workers they would need to help in the German war effort? It made no sense. Surely we were more useful to the Germans alive than dead. It sounded logical. But as efficient and industrious as the Germans were, practicality was not motivating them when it came to the Jews of Europe. Blind, racial hatred was. But we didn't know it, and just couldn't believe it — the Germans wanted us exterminated.

Finally, on May 27, 1944, about two weeks after arriving at the ghetto, our number came up. We were among the last from Dej to come to the ghetto, and now we would be among the first to leave it. The Markovits family would take the first transport from the Bungur Forest to … we didn't know. The guards merely told us we were going to work at an armaments factory that supplied German troops. Once again, we could take only what we were able to carry in our hands. Everything else had to be left behind.

The gates opened. We left the ghetto. It turned out our destination would be the most notorious extermination factory the world has ever known.

# 4

# To the Concentration Camps

Whatever rumours we heard in the past were now irrelevant. Now we would find out our true fate. We walked from the ghetto to the train station, and no, there wasn't a nice passenger train awaiting us. Rather, the guards loaded us into cattle cars, pushing and kicking us like animals, squeezing as many of us as possible into the trains. They had told us at the ghetto to take as many of our belongings as we could hold in our hands or stuff into our pockets. But as soon as we arrived at the train station, they took it all away. Even without our belongings, we were all crammed in so tight there was no room to move. That cliché about sardines in a tin was absolutely true. When the cars were fully packed, the guards closed the doors with a noisy thud, and then locked them with iron bars.

There was another significant difference between the ghetto and the train station. It was Hungarian troops that escorted us out of the ghetto. But at the train station, we were handed over to German soldiers. We noticed the swastikas on their uniforms and guns in hand as they patrolled the platform. Once again, we were told that we were being taken to a labour camp. Which one and where? We had no clue.

The journey by train took several days and it was excruciating. Try to imagine the heat, the hunger, the humiliation. There were no stops along the way. It was next to impossible to sleep. People had to urinate and defecate on the train, crammed up against others. For some, the conditions were too much. They simply died in their places. And there was no way to remove the bodies. People were screaming, crying, and groaning in pain. There were some small openings in the walls to allow in some light and air, but barely anything. On rare occasions, the guards would open the doors and throw in some food and water. It was utterly dehumanizing.

After a few days, the train stopped. We still had no idea where we were. Were we still in Hungary? Then someone from outside screamed in German: "Juden, raus! Schnell!" (Jews, get out! Quickly!). Some people were unable to walk. They were dragged out, and taken away to God only knows where.

A German officer told us to line up in front of the train. And it was at that point that I noticed a sign that read: "Auschwitz." Today, Auschwitz is synonymous with cruelty and death. But to an eleven-year-old boy from Hungary, it meant nothing. I had no knowledge of the frightening reputation of the place. Frankly, I didn't even know what country it was in. Auschwitz, or Oswiecim as it's called in Polish, is more than seven hundred kilometres northwest of Dej, right near Poland's southern border with what was then Czechoslovakia.

We spent the next hour walking from the train station to the concentration camp. There were thick iron gates and German soldiers standing around with guns and dogs, which terrified us even more with their incessant barking. The dogs were huge and vicious. We would frequently hear soldiers tell the dogs in German to "fang ihm" (get him), then unleash the dogs who would attack prisoners. The dogs often drew blood. It was done just for sport.

Although I didn't see it at the time, I gather I was close to what has become one of the most iconic images of the Holocaust — the sign over the entry gate, which held out the promise of freedom, provided we worked hard enough: "Arbeit Macht Frei" (Work Makes You Free). Were we in a labour camp? Maybe the rumours were false and we would survive this horror if we worked hard enough? It was a small shred of hope worth hanging on to.

At this point, my family was still together: my parents, my two sisters, and me. But then, a German official started to sort us into different groups. One of them had a baton in his hand, and directed us on which way to go — women and children to the left, men to the right. Years later, I would come to know that man with the baton as Dr. Josef Mengele, the so-called "Angel of Death," who with the wave of his hand decided who would live and who would die.

My assumption was that we were being separated into different groups in order to perform different tasks, no doubt harder labour for the men, easier work for the women. Even though I was only days away from turning twelve years old and was presumably still regarded by German authorities as a child, I held my father's hand tightly and never let it go. What

I didn't know then was the decision to stay with my father saved my life. Conversely, my two older sisters went with my mother to the left. The selection happened so quickly. Soldiers were screaming at us to move. It was such a chaotic situation, we didn't even have a chance to say goodbye to my mother and sisters. My father suspected this would be the last time we would ever see them alive again.

And it was.

After the selection process was complete, a group of Jews from the camp approached our group. Apparently, it was their job to inform us newcomers of the rules in Auschwitz. All the while, though, they were cursing us in Yiddish.

"Farvos inem gehenem zayn`du kumen aher?" (Why in the hell did you come here?). One would ask. "Zayn nisht du hern der warnings? Du gants are geyn keyn oysgeyn aher." (Didn't you hear the warnings? You all are going to die here).

We were dumbstruck.

They continued. "Du gants are geyn tsu dem crematorium. Dos iz nisht a labour camp. Dos iz a toyt camp keyner leaves dos arayngebn khay" (You all are going to the crematorium. This is not a labour camp. This is a death camp. Nobody leaves this place alive). Then, pointing to the chimneys, they said, "Du vel nayert avekforn dos arayngebn fun ahin" (You will only leave this place from there).

Everything was happening too quickly. We were utterly exhausted after our train transport, starving as well, and barely able to comprehend our circumstances. So our minders explained it all as frankly and bluntly as they could. The selection we had just experienced wasn't about determining who was appropriate for which job. It was a selection for life or death. All those who turned to the left were now on their way to the crematorium, they told us. They were being escorted to their deaths at this very moment, including our rabbi from Dej, the one who told my father to stay in the ghetto as that represented his best chance at survival.

Did we believe it? Even after everything we'd experienced, I think there was still a part of us that found it impossible to believe. Why kill us? Didn't they need us? But the reality of Auschwitz began to dawn on us. And there was an incident that took place as we got off the train that gave an indication of the hell we had just entered.

As the guards were sorting people, some of those soldiers decided to have a little "fun," no doubt bored with their circumstances. Or perhaps one of the little babies was crying too loudly, and its mother couldn't stop the child from sobbing. Regardless of the reason, one soldier took the child from its mother, and began a "game" that every loving parent plays with their little kids — tossing the child up in the air and catching it. If you've done it, you'll know it can quickly turn tears into laughter. But the Germans changed the rules of the game. As one soldier threw the child in the air, the others — all SS soldiers — used the baby as target practice. They shot the child in mid-air. It all happened before our disbelieving eyes. If we had any illusions about what lay ahead for us in Auschwitz, those illusions should have collapsed at that moment. And yet, we still wanted to believe — needed to believe — that somehow we would survive all this.

As an aside, let me relate an incident that happened many years later with my oldest son. Moshe had to write an essay for school and the story of the SS officers killing this defenseless child was the story he chose to tell. Moshe had heard me speak of this event over the years. The teacher said the essay was fine but that there was a problem with Moshe's imagination. The teacher appended a note to the essay, saying Moshe didn't need to so dramatically embellish what was obviously a fictitious story. I guess I could forgive the teacher for her views. All these years later, it's still hard to believe I saw what I saw. Can human beings really be that cruel to each other? To a harmless baby?

I went to Moshe's school to meet the teacher, not to chastise or criticize her, or even to justify what Moshe had written. Rather, I needed to tell the teacher that these things really had happened. I needed her to expand her understanding of history. To this day, I really don't know whether the teacher believed me or not. If you were raised in the latter half of the twentieth century in peaceful Canada, why would you believe such stories? How could you not conclude that this parent was exaggerating? But as I tell people, just because something is too horrible to believe doesn't mean it didn't happen.

In any event, the *kapos* took us into the Auschwitz concentration camp. I stayed close to my father and went into the barracks. We were ordered to remove our clothes, throw them in a pile on the floor, and put on the camp uniform. All the while I wondered if my mother was still alive. Were my sisters? Or had they already gone to the gas chambers? Were their bodies already en route to the crematoria for burning? Such horrifying thoughts.

We spent several dreadful days in Auschwitz. They seemed to separate us into our ethnic nationalities. We were grouped with other Hungarians. Eventually, our uniforms would indicate why we had been sent here. Jews had one particular symbol on our clothes; political prisoners another; homosexuals another; and so on.

And the selection for the crematoria wasn't over yet. While women and young children, especially daughters, were the first to go, next came a second selection of young boys who may have been unfit for hard labour. We received instructions that all children over the age of thirteen could stay, but that anyone younger than thirteen was to be moved elsewhere to a "special camp." By now, we knew all too well what that meant: gas chambers and crematoria. My father and I started plotting how we could keep me alive. I simply didn't look tall enough to pass for thirteen, so we searched for whatever we could and stuffed it into my shoes to make me look taller. When the Germans were around, I kept my shoulders back, and my neck stretched up, again to convey the impression that I was older and taller than I really was. It worked.

At this point, I need to tell you about a bittersweet surprise we experienced at Auschwitz. Remember, we had no knowledge of where my two older brothers were. By being at the yeshiva, they avoided the Dej ghetto and subsequent transport to Auschwitz. However, I would later learn that the boys were sent from the yeshiva to a Hungarian labour camp with other Jews. That camp was established by the regime of Miklós Horthy de Nagybánya. His title was "His Serene Highness, the Regent of the Kingdom of Hungary." Horthy remains a divisive figure in Hungarian history. His close relations with Nazi Germany allowed him to reclaim lands lost to Hungary through various treaties. But the

Nazis eventually soured on him because they found him insufficiently committed to the Final Solution — the extermination of European Jewry. By the spring of 1944, Germany lost patience with Horthy, invaded Hungary, and essentially took control of the country. In October, Horthy was placed under arrest, and taken to Bavaria, where he remained until the end of the war.

To avoid one of Horthy's labour camps, both Dudi and Shuli escaped to the bigger cities to avoid the attention of suspicious neighbours; Dudi hid in Budapest and Shuli hid in Debrecen. For a time, they were relatively safe as the Hungarian authorities had not pursued Jews there. But eventually, their luck ran out and they were swept up, taken to a ghetto, and then, like us, sent to Auschwitz. So, by the time my parents, sisters, and I arrived at Auschwitz, my brothers were already there, although because they came separately, neither knew the other was there. When Dudi heard through the grapevine that a transport from Dej had arrived at the camp, he began to look for us.

Somehow, one day, he snuck out of his cell block, traversed the camp, and got access to our barracks. I have to confess, when I first saw Dudi, I didn't recognize him. He looked so utterly different from how I recalled him. Remember, he left home in 1940 and I rarely saw him after that. Now, his formerly thick, long hair was all gone. His head was shaved, as Auschwitz regulations required.

Dudi recognized me and told me what I had to do to escape the crematorium. "Motke, du muzn oysbahaltn funem selections un alts blaybn mit tateh" (You must hide from the selections and always stay with father), he told me. It was the only time I saw him in Auschwitz, but I followed his advice, and it saved my life. When the guards or *kapos* called us to line up in front of the barracks, I would hide and refuse to come out, or sneak into another barracks. I'd move from one to another, desperately trying to stay ahead of the authorities as they checked inside. I also scouted out other places where I could hide. During the night, I wouldn't stay in the barracks because you never knew — there could be an unexpected selection, and then I would be caught off guard. The safest place I could find to hide was in the yard near the bathrooms, where all the dead bodies were brought and piled up, one upon another. As appalling as this sounds, I would get on to that pile, lie down next to the dead bodies and pretend I was one of them. It worked.

Life in Auschwitz, if you can call it that, consisted of simply trying to stay alive for one more day. We had very little food and suffered from hunger all the time. Essentially, there was one evening meal a day and to call it a meal wasn't quite accurate. It was a bowl of soupy mush, maybe some potatoes, and that was it. They usually gave us food in barrels, which was an advantage for a little guy like me. When the barrel was empty, it was thrown away, but it still contained some food left at the bottom that the adults were unable to reach. I could get inside the barrel, and scrape the leftovers from the bottom. In this way, my dad and I got some extra food.

We were in Auschwitz for almost two weeks. My father and I worked in a cement factory with a few hundred other prisoners. I was basically the water boy. What I remember most from that time is the sense of horror and danger that haunted me every minute I was there. It's impossible to forget the tall chimneys with dark, thick smoke rising out of them. And the dogs barking, always barking. But there were other absurdities that, for some reason, stay with me. I recall seeing two kids, probably about my age, being escorted every morning outside the camp to clean the officers' houses. They were always escorted by a couple of armed guards. How bizarre it was to see those big guys leading two scrawny, small boys at gunpoint. With all of the death I saw in Auschwitz, why does that image stay with me? Who knows?

Do you know what it's like to spend every waking moment of your life simply thinking of how to stay alive? I hope not. No one should live under such circumstances. But that's the way it was. I used all my wits and took advice from whoever would offer it to remain alive. And I prayed. Yes, there was prayer, even in Auschwitz. The first thing I did every morning was say the Shema, the Hebrew prayer acknowledging God's oneness. ("Hear O Israel, the Lord our God, the Lord is one.") I said it just to myself, never out loud. However, at least three times a day in the barracks, or when there was a spare moment, someone who knew the prayers by heart would sing and we would follow along. That's another image that stays with me: a crowd of prisoners in their white and black striped uniforms, huddled together, singing, praying, and begging God to save them. Don't ask me how, but amazingly, my father managed to sneak his *tefillin* into Auschwitz. If you don't know what they are, *tefillin* are phylacteries — two small, black leather boxes that are worn on the head and arm, containing verses from the Torah. Orthodox Jewish men put on their *tefillin* every morning (except the Sabbath) and they're considered among the most important and holy items for praying. The boxes have long, black straps attached to them. One box goes on the arm, with the straps wrapped around the bicep, forearm, and hand in a special fashion. The second box is worn on the forehead at the hairline, with its straps going around the back of the head, connected at the top of the neck with a special knot, and hanging in front on each side. My father no doubt was risking death if his *tefillin* were ever discovered during one of the searches. And yet, he did it. That alone shows how much significance he placed on those items and his faith in God. Like so many of our other possessions, I have no idea what happened to those *tefillin*.

Did I ever pray to God to get us out of this death camp? Strangely enough, I don't recall ever doing that. It never occurred to me to ask God to save our lives. I didn't blame God for putting us in this predicament, so maybe that's why I didn't ask for his help in getting us out.

Near the end of our time at Auschwitz — I'm not sure exactly when; keeping track of time was not an exact science there — we got word that we would soon be taken to another camp, and the administration began segmenting us into new groups. But this hardly meant we were in the clear. I still feared being selected for death, and those selection teams did continue to do their "work." So I spent another couple of days in hiding. Then, finally, the death camp gates opened up, and we walked out. Given the carnage that we had seen over the intervening two weeks, we were incredibly lucky to get out of there alive. I began to wonder whether God had some special plan for me.

We began our next march, from Auschwitz to Birkenau. Birkenau was one of forty sub-camps in the Auschwitz complex.

It was just a few kilometres away from the main Auschwitz camp, in another town called Zasole. It's estimated that 90 percent of the prisoners who died in the Auschwitz complex were Jews — that's one million Jewish souls that were destroyed there. And there were tens of thousands more from other ethnic groups who also perished: Poles, Soviets, Yugoslavs, French, Austrians, and Roma (called Gypsies then). It was as efficient a killing machine as the world has ever known. We walked, several hundred of us for a couple of hours, from Auschwitz to Birkenau, and then south to the Mauthausen-Gusen concentration camp just east of Linz, in northern Austria. Even though I was the youngest of the group, by this point, I had stopped worrying about being selected for death. In Mauthausen, we changed clothes and I got a uniform that was actually my size. Everything I had worn before was too big for me. But once again, after just two days in Mauthausen, we were on the move. We were then transported to Gusen-I, a nearby labour camp. This really was a labour camp; the danger of the gas chambers was apparently behind us. We were placed in barracks again, and my dad and I were in Number 7. We got our hair cut in a particular way — a line shaved in the middle of the head to show that the inmate belonged to this camp.

My father and I shared a bunk bed again — him on the top, me on the bottom. We got assigned to different groups to work different jobs. My father was in the cement brigade. I was left in the camp to clean the barracks. Every barrack had a capacity of two hundred people. In the morning, before the sun was up, we would line up outside the building and be counted. It was called the morning *appel* (from the French word for call). We had to go out half-naked and wash under the open skies, regardless of the weather, although we were "lucky" in the sense that it was summertime and the weather wasn't too harsh. The water was ice cold and of course there was no soap. Then we returned to our barracks and made the beds with thin mattresses and blankets. The bodies of those who died overnight would be taken out and carried away. We then had to line up outside again and again. And the SS guards, clad in their gray uniforms with black boots, were so sadistic. There would be fifty of them with dogs, pistols, and rifles. If someone wasn't lined up just perfectly straight, they'd think nothing of unleashing one of their vicious dogs to attack the prisoner. I saw a dog chew open a man's stomach once. They'd also let the dogs attack you if you were caught sleeping on the job. Or if you missed your *appel.* We would line up literally for three to four hours at a time, just standing there, with no talking, of course. It happened day or night. If someone was missing, we'd all be forced to continue standing until they found him, and when they did, it was twenty-five lashes to the back with the whip.

SS officers would come and we called out our numbers: "Block One," "Block Two," "Block Seven," and so on. The block leader told us to take our hats off for inspection and be ready. And after that, every group went to its respective workplace.

When people came back from work, it was time for the evening meal. The food distribution was hell. We had to wait in a straight line, and if any of those very hungry people walked out of the line, the guards would beat the hell out of them. I remember one incident when a guy from my hometown, just a couple years older than me, stepped out of line. He was probably so hungry that he couldn't wait anymore and tried to take some food. One of the *kapos* took a hammer and struck him with all his might, right on the head. The poor man's brains literally fell out of his skull and blood was everywhere. His name was Nahmi. I can remember this scene with such vividness, it's as if it happened just yesterday. It was the first time I had witnessed an adult killed right before my eyes. I had seen plenty of dead people before: on the transport to Auschwitz, in the barracks at Auschwitz, and of course, that baby killed at our arrival at Auschwitz. But even that episode — seen at a distance, my senses numb from the long, exhausting train transport — didn't affect me as much as this brutal murder right before my eyes. And it was someone I knew. It was a painful reminder that, even though the gas chambers may have been behind us, nothing had changed. Life could be snuffed out at any moment. Every day, someone died in our barracks. Death was an all too familiar sight. As I recall these days, part of me still can't believe this all happened.

Why didn't more people try to escape? Well, actually, they did, although I never heard of anyone successfully making the attempt. Every morning there were dead bodies along the barbwire fences around the camp. The electrified fences instantly killed anyone who touched them. Everybody knew they were electrified and yet, they were so desperate, so hopeless, perhaps it was simply an act of suicide. Those deaths never stopped.

Prisoners tried to escape in other ways too. The most hopeful approach was to slip away from a work crew outside the camp. If that prisoner was caught, we would all find out about it soon enough. They would be put to death and their bodies put on display all day long as a lesson to others.

However, if someone did succeed in an escape, it meant added hardship and suffering for the rest of us. The Germans would shoot an entire group of prisoners to show us that resistance was futile, and escaping would be costly. Sometimes, a prisoner or two would pretend to fall asleep, hoping to escape when the guards left. In that case, the entire group would stand in line outside the barracks waiting for the Germans to find the "sleepyheads." We sometimes would stand in place for hours. The Nazis took attendance twice a day to make sure that everyone was present. Their penchant for bureaucratic efficiency was well known, even when it came to putting Jews to death. Years later, I had a chance to see just how meticulous they were when I saw documents that proved I was, indeed, a prisoner in the Nazi camps. The documents described everything: when I was taken; what camps I was in; how I was transported there; how long I was kept there; and what my duties were. It was astonishing.

In Gusen, which housed twelve to seventeen thousand prisoners, two Polish gentiles actually helped me enormously and made my life better. They were political prisoners working in the camp as *kapos* in charge of our barrack, and they were kind to me. They asked me my name. I told them it was Moritz. When one of them asked whether I was Jewish, I confirmed that I was. They advised me, going forward, that whenever I was asked about my nationality, I should simply say I was half-Jewish. The older one of the two, whose name was Yatsek, said he had a son that was my age, and he promised to take care of me as if I were his own child. They would secretly give me extra food on the condition that I promise only to share it with my father and nobody else. They were disobeying regulations and knew they could be severely punished if caught. Nevertheless, I saw so much misery around me, I couldn't help but share some of what they gave me with others. I suspect my stomach had shrunk from lack of food, and I simply didn't need much to get by. Fortunately, no one found out.

Some of these concentration camp habits I actually still practice today, for example, refraining from finishing all my food in one sitting — saving some of it for later. I can't really explain why I still do this, but I do. I just got into the habit, while in concentration camps, of only eating half my bread, and secretly saving the rest for later.

There weren't many non-Jews who were helpful to me during my imprisonment, but I shall never forget those that were. They no doubt contributed to the fact that I am still alive today.

Gusen-II was considered one of the harshest of all the German penal camps. And yet, I remember a German soldier (from the Wehrmacht, not the notoriously cruel SS) who gave me some extra food and explained he was doing so because he also had a son around my age. As a father, he just couldn't abide seeing children suffering around him without feeling compassion. By this time, I had improved my German significantly and we were able to understand each other. So there were occasional incidents of humanity in these concentration camps. But it was unexpected and rare.

The labour in Gusen-II was incredibly difficult and I began to suspect my father, who wasn't yet fifty years old, wouldn't last long. He was so sick, and depressed at the loss of my mother and two sisters, he simply didn't want to live anymore. He had lost the will. He felt his life was worthless and meaningless. But he told me I was young and had a good chance of surviving.

"You must, for the sake of our family, get through all of this and live," he told me. "Then find a way to get to Israel, where we will meet again."

Toward the end of 1944, I can't remember the precise date, my father told me he simply couldn't go to work anymore. When it came time for the morning count, he refused to let me help him come outside. I knew it was over for him and begged to join him. I just didn't want to be left alone, to live life without him. Besides, the *kapos* said the regulations didn't allow for that anyway. I asked the *kapos* to bring me some of my father's ashes so I could keep a part of him with me. This wasn't permitted either. The *kapos* took my father away, and I never saw him again. This was the only time I can recall myself crying.

I now felt totally alone in the world. The death camps of Nazi Germany had claimed the lives of both of my parents, both of my sisters, and for all I knew, my brothers were gone too. I had two stark options: give up and give way to the worst evil the world had ever known, or somehow gather the strength to persevere. I made a decision.

I decided to survive.

In the days ahead, I noticed a difference in the new arrivals at Gusen-II. They came wearing civilian clothes, rather than the Auschwitz "uniform." It suggested to us that the smooth functioning of the extermination machine was breaking down. The rumours we had heard about Soviet troops moving closer to concentration camps must have been true.

I stayed in Gusen-II until February 1945. I worked as a water boy, bringing water to the work sites. I cleaned houses for German officers. My situation had improved a little as the officers let me eat their leftovers. It was much better food than the ration we had in the camp. But those soldiers also knew where this war was heading. They could see the inevitable end. What must have been going through their minds? Did they ever appreciate the horror for which they were responsible? Did they fear retribution? Once again, I experienced a rare moment of kindness as they told me they were confident I would survive. They encouraged me to hold on until it was all over. I wondered whether their compassion, so late in the game, was genuine or perhaps motivated by their own fears of what their futures held. If they weren't afraid of the vengeance that could be coming for them for their unspeakable crimes, they should have been.

But the Nazi concentration camp system wasn't quite finished with me yet. In February 1945, I was moved to yet another camp: Gunskirchen, also in Upper Austria. Once again, death was everywhere. We had to march on foot for two days to get to that camp, and many were killed along the way, especially those too weak or sick to walk —they were simply shot on the spot. As always, I was the youngest in my group of several hundred.

Gunskirchen was a terrible camp. Its construction started in December 1944 and it was intended to house only a few hundred slave labourers. However, once the so-called "death marches" from Mauthausen-Gusen were undertaken, thousands upon thousands of us showed up at Gunskirchen. Some seventeen thousand Hungarian Jews were thought to have passed through the camp. Typhus and dysentery were everywhere. There were only German guards, no *kapos*, and almost no food. Women also lived in the camp but in different sections.

It was in Gunskirchen that I witnessed one of the most horrible sights imaginable: starving people eating human flesh. It was apparent that people had simply lost their minds. The most basic of human, moral standards had disintegrated under the yoke of months of inhuman treatment. The place was just packed. Prisoners were happy when a fellow inmate died. They'd throw the body out the window, which meant more space for the survivors. Every dead man represented a little more space, a little more air, a little more bread for the rest of us. What madness had befallen us, to the point where we welcomed death because it offered hope to the rest of us?

The world was as perverted as anything I could imagine. But I hung on to the hope that this perversion would soon be over.

# 5

# Liberation

We had heard rumours that it would be the Soviet Red Army that would liberate us from Gunskirchen. In fact, it was the Americans and Canadians. And the German soldiers must have known the U.S. Army was coming because I saw them toss away their uniforms and weapons and leave the camp. I instantly knew what was going on, and so I quit the camp as well. Others came out with me. It was a totally surreal feeling. After all the armed supervision, humiliation, and near brushes with death, our incarceration ended, frankly, with an absence of drama. We just walked through the gates; nobody was guarding them anymore. Germany's finest and most brutal soldiers had all gone into hiding. Some even tried mixing in with the prisoners in order to fool the liberating allied troops. All of the Nazis' brutally efficient concentration camp operations simply stopped functioning.

With a new sense of freedom, we wandered to places surrounding our camp, trying to find food and clothing. Everything in the surrounding town of Linz had been abandoned — banks, jewelry stores, post offices were all open, but no one was inside. People could literally walk in and take whatever they wanted, and many did. They grabbed paper money by the sack load, and looted jewelry as well. My sense was that the prisoners were probably in the minority among those participating in the lootings; most were local residents taking advantage of a lawless situation. Other locals quietly sat behind their locked doors, but when prisoners knocked and asked for help, they would open up and give whatever assistance was requested. Even though they didn't participate directly in the Nazis' crimes, they did seem quite concerned that we would retaliate against them. But we didn't.

I was in the company of two older Jewish men, and the first thing I remember doing was knocking on a local resident's door and asking for permission to take a shower. After so many cold washes outside barracks after barracks, it was heavenly to stand under a stream of hot water, then dry myself with a towel. Imagine, nearly a year without ever feeling clean. Imagine a year of suffering constant bodily abuse. Imagine a year of constantly thinking, this is my last day on earth. Surely I will be killed today. But somehow, miraculously, I wasn't.

The owners treated us to whatever they could find in their kitchens. Was it out of fear? Or perhaps guilt? No matter, they gave us whatever we asked for. We weren't oppressive in our demands. We simply wanted some food and some clothes — anything other than the hated black and white striped prison uniforms we wore at the time.

We also learned how unpredictably the human body can react after it's been denied the basics of life, month after month, and year after year. Since many houses were empty, many starving prisoners simply broke in, searching for anything they could get their hands on to eat. It was a huge mistake. Some gorged themselves on rich foods, which their bodies simply couldn't process. I watched someone grab an entire bar of butter and swallow it whole. His body convulsed and he died right in front of me. Their behavior was totally irrational, bordering on suicidal, but they had no control of themselves. They just seemed incapable of listening to the voice of reason telling them not to do that.

Of course, I understood their madness. Who would dare judge such people? They had witnessed and experienced some of the worst depravity in human history. How does one emerge from that horror and remain "normal"? Would we ever feel "normal" again? Could we? Many took to alcoholic binges, hoping the booze would dull their senses and make the pain go away. I couldn't blame them.

Even though the guards had disappeared, some prisoners refused to leave their concentration camps. They wanted vengeance first. They picked up weapons that had been abandoned by the guards and began hunting for their tormentors. When they came upon a member of the dreaded SS, those Nazis were killed without hesitation. Nobody was going to shed a tear for those barbarians. They deserved to be shot without trial or discussion. Same for anyone in a German troop uniform or those *kapos* who had collaborated with the Nazis and abused inmates. Some of them were even worse than the SS officers. I also saw other German tormenters hanged by the soon-to-be former prisoners and set afire. Once the U.S. soldiers did arrive, they took control of the situation and restored order. They began to identify all of the concentration camp inmates and offered assistance in returning to home, or finding a new way in life.

They offered me an opportunity to immigrate to the United States. There was a rabbi with the American troops and when I told him that I was Jewish he asked if I knew any prayers. Of course, I remembered many prayers by heart. I recited some from the Book of Psalms. He offered to help me move to America, and if I wanted, he would start working on my immigration papers.

Frankly, I didn't know what to do. His offer was very generous. I was under the assumption that all of my family had been put to death and I was all that remained of our original family from Dej. I had heard nothing from Dudi since our brief meeting in Auschwitz, and assumed both he and Shuli were dead. The fact that I was alive was astonishing enough, I thought. Could there be three miracles in one family? I doubted it. In fact, I doubted that anyone from our community in Dej had survived. So, returning to Dej was a non-starter. That was not an option. But America? All I could remember at this point was my father's dying wish that I go to Israel and start over. So that was it. I resolved to do that. I had to keep my word to my dad.

But before that, some political prisoners from Poland suggested that I come with them to see whether we could find any Jewish survivors I knew that had ended up in Poland. I agreed, and so I joined them and went to the city of Lodz, where I stayed for several months. Again, remember, this was 1945. There was no mass media to speak of, and so word of mouth was how we got our "news." One of the things I heard was that someone named Markovits, a former resident of Dej, was alive. My hopes soared, but of course, history taught me not to get too excited. Who knew how true these rumours might be?

I began searching and searching and soon, against all odds, I discovered that the man from Dej was my brother Shuli. Could it really be true? Somehow, we got in touch with each other — all these years later, I don't remember how — and we met in Budapest. It was only when I saw him with my own eyes that I believed he really was alive. I think he was even more shocked than I was. I was probably the youngest of the Jewish children from Dej who had survived the Holocaust. Maybe some thirteen or fourteen year olds managed to survive the concentration camps, but nobody who was just eleven.

So now there were two of us. But what about Dudi? Shuli knew nothing of what happened to him. So we kept searching, asking others, listening to stories, getting in touch with Jewish organizations, and doing whatever we could to find any clues as to his whereabouts.

Then, six months after my liberation, we got the news that our oldest brother Dudi was also alive. But the news wasn't completely positive. Apparently, he was sick with typhus, in very serious condition, but thankfully improving. Shuli found a way to contact him, and we all decided to meet back in our hometown of Dej, which of course was now in Romania.

As I think back on this time, it really was amazing that we managed to track each other down. Today, people who haven't seen each other in thirty years send out a message on Facebook and they're instantly reconnected. But back then, we had no such advanced methods of communication. It was a painstaking process of following up on leads or getting the word out through officials. We would also put up notices on bulletin boards or building walls at street level. It was very much like taking a shot in the dark, but surprisingly, these techniques occasionally worked. So if you're wondering why it would take six months to find someone, that's why!

A frequent occurrence for Holocaust survivors was to go back to their hometowns and see what had become of their former homes. Shuli and I did the same. For many survivors, they knew moving back into their homes was impossible. Local non-Jewish residents had already claimed those homes as their own, despite the fact that legally, those homes should still have been ours and the locals no doubt paid nothing for them. They were squatters, but there was nothing the survivors could do about it. In fact, in some cases, even many years after the war, Jews simply wanted to see what had become of their former homes, but were intimidated or even murdered by local residents, who feared we were attempting to reclaim our former properties. This wasn't the case.

And it certainly was not on our agenda either. Yes, Shuli and I saw the home in which we grew up in Dej, but it was occupied by a Hungarian or Romanian family living there. We weren't looking for trouble, so we rented an apartment, and began to wait for Dudi to arrive.

I should add that Shuli was a dramatically changed person after the war. He was angry — very angry. I think were he to be diagnosed today, doctors would have concluded he suffered from post-traumatic stress disorder (PTSD). The horrors of spending so much time in Auschwitz took a vicious toll on him.

Nevertheless, to our joy and disbelief, all three brothers were reunited in Dej. The rest of our happy family had been destroyed. But we were alive. We shared our respective stories of survival. I was anxious to learn how Dudi and Shuli initially managed to avoid being sent to Auschwitz. What I learned I could scarcely believe. My brothers apparently outsmarted the vaunted, efficient, ultra-bureaucratic German soldiers, almost by playing a game on the authorities. In fact, the Nazis' slavish attention to detail may ultimately have been what kept my brothers alive. The authorities in Hungary were determined to transport as many Jews to Auschwitz as they could, but regulations required that they go in chronological order — the older before the younger. So my brothers literally swapped identification documents at key moments while still living in Hungary. Whenever the authorities came for my older brother Dudi, he took his younger brother Shuli's papers. Incredibly, the soldiers didn't realize they were being tricked and backed off, leaving Dudi alone. This worked for quite some time. At some point, my brothers decided not to press their luck with this scheme any further, and Dudi decided to go into hiding in Budapest and Shuli in Debrecen.

Eventually, their luck did run out, and Shuli was captured by the gendarmes and taken to the local ghetto in Debrecen, which became home to the more than ten thousand Jews. Before long, he began discussing the possibility of escaping with some other young people. They waited for just the right moment and then left the ghetto unnoticed. The plan was to get to Romania where Jews were reportedly being treated much better than in Hungary, even though the Romanians were also allies of Germany. Shuli's group took a train to get out of Debrecen, but then something happened that proved the times for Jews had changed dramatically for the worse.

Some of the other passengers on the train became suspicious of Shuli's group and reported to the train's authorities that a curious looking group of youngsters was aboard. At the next station, the gendarmes were waiting for them. My brother and his friends were plucked off the train and sent immediately to Auschwitz.

As strange as it sounds, Shuli was lucky. He was young and strong and therefore selected to do hard labour (as opposed to being sent to the gas chambers immediately). Like they did with me, some of his fellow inmates who had been in Auschwitz longer than he told him, while pointing to the chimneys, that that was the only way out of Auschwitz.

Shuli also saw the notorious Dr. Josef Mengele, clad in white gloves, holding his baton, selecting those who would live a while longer, while others were sent to his lab to be subjects of his horrifying medical experiments. Patients were never informed what was in store for them. In fact, Mengele's torture chamber resulted in disfigurement, permanent disability, or death for his "patients."

Shuli told me he soon learned the only way to survive Auschwitz was to be good at some craft or trade. That could buy you some additional time. So even though he'd never done any painting in the past, he presented himself as an experienced painter. He was appointed to a team of painters, and tattooed with a number on his arm — an "honour" that was only awarded to permanent residents of Auschwitz. (Fortunately, I wasn't there long enough to merit such a tattoo). Shuli worked outside the camp, for example, painting military hospitals for German officers.

However, at one point, Shuli was taken off his painting detail and assigned to the most dreaded job — a *sonderkommando.* These were prisoners whose duty it was to prepare new camp arrivals for gassing. Refusal to accept this burden meant instant death. The *sonderkommandos* helped the victims take off their clothes and surrender their personal possessions. Then, after the mass execution was over, they had to transfer the corpses from the gas chambers to the ovens. But before that, the corpses were put through one last bit of dehumanizing treatment. The *sonderkommandos* had to extract any gold that the victims may have had in their teeth. What a monstrous task.

Being a *sonderkommando* also usually meant your days were numbered. Doing the job drained you of your physical and emotional strength. Even with a death sentence staring you in the face if you failed to co-operate, how could you not feel inhumane? The Nazis rotated the *sonderkommandos* through this job every two weeks, which meant forty new people were regularly required. And they didn't want any witnesses to their evil deeds to remain, so the *sonderkommandos* were also put to death after their usefulness had run out. The authorities asked for volunteers but if there weren't enough, they would simply choose anyone they wanted.

Just before he sensed his time was up, Shuli escaped from his barracks and went to the women's section of the camp.

Fortunately, nobody noticed him and the women hid him until the threat of being assigned yet again to the *sonderkommandos* was gone.

I'm not sure how the prisoners knew, but Yom Kippur in 1944 arrived on September 27 at sunset. Yom Kippur, the Day of Atonement, is the holiest day on the Jewish calendar. It's the day we ask God to forgive us for all of our sins. So on September 28, when the prisoners in Shuli's barracks were called to line up in front of their building, someone whispered, "It's Yom Kippur. Let's sing. Whoever can sing, go ahead." Shuli, who always had a beautiful voice, took up the offer. The Nazis did not appreciate either his voice or his bravery. They considered the spectacle of Jews praying in a death camp to be too provocative, and so they attacked the poor prisoners, beating and kicking them furiously. In the ensuing chaos and panic, Shuli escaped to one of the other barracks in the camp and hid under somebody's bunk. The bunk was so small that Shuli was barely able to squeeze himself underneath it. He spent two days there, hiding until he felt it might be safe to come out and return to his own barracks. By then, his place had been taken by another prisoner, so he had to find a new bunk for himself. Once again, my brother barely cheated death.

I always felt Shuli had the worst time out of all us three brothers. He stayed in Auschwitz (the only concentration camp in which he was imprisoned) from March or April of 1944 until December 1944 or January 1945. When the Soviet army approached the place, the Germans decided to evacuate the remaining prisoners and Shuli was part of a group forced into a "Death March" to somewhere else. Many of the sick and weak were shot by German troops if they were unable to keep up the pace. Hunger took its share of prisoners along the way as well. Sometimes when the prisoners passed villages or farms, some compassionate souls gave away a piece of bread or potatoes.

Shuli expressed his surprise when he saw tanks of soldiers coming. When the soldiers disembarked, he heard British soldiers speaking Yiddish, and then Hebrew. It was the Jewish Brigade, a military formation of the British Army that was recruited from Palestine.

Dudi got to Auschwitz about the same time as Shuli, but he was transported from the Budapest ghetto, so evidently they ended up in different sections of the camp and did not realize until afterward that they were there at the same time. Remember, more than a million Jews were put to death in Auschwitz, not to mention 150,000 Poles and more than 20,000 Roma. So the notion that we might all be there at the same time but not know it was quite understandable.

In Budapest, Dudi had met a young woman named Olga and they began to make plans for the future when the round-ups for the ghetto began. Dudi eventually managed to escape the ghetto and find shelter in a synagogue outside Budapest. But how crazy was this — the local Jews eventually refused to provide cover for him and asked him to leave. Even worse, they reported him to the authorities, and he was brought back to the ghetto. Maybe they thought by selling my brother out, they'd ingratiate themselves with the local authorities and perhaps inoculate themselves from the pending disaster. I doubt it worked.

Later, Dudi was on the same train as Olga and her family, all of them deported to Auschwitz. The Germans, of course, separated him and Olga during the selection, and he believed it was over for them. He threw a handkerchief over to his girlfriend as a final symbol of his love for her, and shouted that they would never see each other again. He was sure that Olga was taken to the gas chambers. But Dudi was young and strong, and for that reason he was selected for labour. As I mentioned earlier, while in Auschwitz, Dudi had heard that a train was coming from Dej. He somehow managed to infiltrate our ranks long enough to meet me and urge me to stay as close to our father as possible, to avoid being selected for the gas chambers. That advice proved to be invaluable.

While he was in the labour camp, Dudi was first assigned to collect unexploded bombs left after air raids. But he only had to see some of his fellow prisoners blown to bits by these ordnances a few times before asking for a different job. For some reason, they consented to his request and sent him to a construction site. That assignment turned out to be just as dangerous if not worse than the bomb-defusing job. People would fall to their deaths from the high walls while working. So Dudi tried a different strategy and found success in … a toilet. In the morning, instead of going to his workplace, he would sneak into the bathrooms and hide there. He always kept a hammer with him, to make it look as if he were en route to a jobsite. If someone from the camp administration entered, he made himself look busy by pretending to fix the facilities.

Hanging out in the bathrooms or getting a job in them was a clever strategy for survival. Because the bathrooms were infested with disease and unbearable odours, the German officers and guards avoided them. In addition, bathroom breaks were extremely infrequent for prisoners, so by working in the bathrooms, access when you wanted it wasn't an issue.

That strategy of my brother's worked for some time until one German officer caught on and exposed his avoidance of work. Normally, that would have meant an instant execution, if only to set an example for the other prisoners. But for some reason — again, no one knows why — the officer covered for him. Once again, Dudi cheated death. And it wouldn't be the last time. But it was an extraordinary accomplishment. The average lifespan of an Auschwitz prisoner was two weeks.

On another occasion at another camp, Dudi tried to escape but was captured. Unlike in Auschwitz where death was the only possible sentence, he was offered a choice: either take a bullet or the lash. He chose the lashes, took twenty-five hits, and for a few days was virtually unable to stand or walk.

But he was alive.

On another occasion, he was even closer to death. There was a selection in his labour camp, supposedly for some industrial purposes. But someone tipped him off that all Jews who were to be selected would actually be going not to work, but rather to be exterminated. Dudi was told if he wanted to save his life, he had to avoid that selection. So Dudi found a way to mix with a group of French prisoners and pretended that he was one of them, which wasn't particularly easy since he didn't speak any French. He helped give the impression he was one of the French prisoners by stealing a coat from one of them. The coat had a special marking identifying the country, and Dudi simply acted as someone who was very depressed and therefore reluctant to communicate with his compatriots. Those fingered in the next selection were, in fact, taken away to their deaths, while Dudi and the other French prisoners were loaded onto a train and transported to a new place.

That trip was long, with little food. Guards would occasionally open the doors and kick something in for the prisoners to eat. They would never "serve" the Jews with their hands, as that was somehow debasing to the soldiers. As always, many starved and died along the way, and Dudi, as I did, witnessed horrific episodes of people eating human flesh to survive. They cut slices of tissue from the dead, and spooned the blood trickling from the wounds. Finally, the group arrived at Dachau, the first prison camp built in Germany, about sixteen kilometres northwest of Munich. Eventually, on April 29, 1945, Dudi and his fellow prisoners were liberated by American troops. The liberators were so appalled by what they saw in Dachau that they executed as many as fifty guards and members of the camp administration on the spot, even though those criminals were prepared to surrender to the Americans. Dudi helped find and expose some Nazis who tried to hide among the prisoners by wearing prison uniforms. But that was hard for SS soldiers to do, since they had an unmistakable identification mark — a blood group insignia, tattooed in the armpit. The tattoo was intended to save their lives if they were wounded in fighting, unconscious, and unable to provide information to their doctors. A glance at this sign would tell the medical staff what blood type was needed for a transfusion. Now the same sign positively identified them as war criminals.

After his liberation, Dudi immediately started searching for any information about his girlfriend Olga. He didn't have much hope of finding her alive. The chances of women surviving the death camps were not high. But miraculously, Dudi found Olga in Munich, and there was reason to celebrate in spite of everything they had gone through.

So there we were, we three brothers, in Dej, with a serious decision to make. We had just endured unspeakable horrors, all because of our religion. So we discussed whether to keep our Jewish identity or abandon it. After all, if these tragedies happened once, they could happen again. There was only one reason why we were targeted for extermination: we were Jews. We knew anti-Semitism had been around for millennia, and in all likelihood would continue well into the future. All it would take was another obsessed, manipulative dictator for us to be targets once again. Was it worth the risk to remain Jews? Now that this war was over, we all wanted to marry, have families, and just lead normal lives. Would it be fair to our progeny to subject them to the risks and horrors we had just endured? Wouldn't it be better to protect them by choosing a different name, ethnicity, and way of life?

As you might imagine, these were intense conversations for someone of my age. I was only thirteen years old and my brothers were barely into their twenties. We discussed it every day while staying in Dej. We tried to weigh all the pros and cons, considered the history, and our possible futures. We had just escaped from hell and shuddered at the thought that future generations of Markovitses would have to endure similar experiences.

But I could never get the words my father told me out of my head. "Go to Israel," he said. I just couldn't betray his trust, his love, and his hopes for me.

I just couldn't stop being Jewish.

So we three brothers decided to be loyal to our heritage, our parents, our religion, and our roots. We feared the risks could be high. But at the end of the day, there really wasn't any other option. We simply couldn't live with ourselves unless we were Jewish. And we figured the best place in the world to be Jewish was Israel.

That belief was tested in excruciating fashion.

# 6

# On to Israel

Our life in eastern Europe was over. After more than a century, the Jewish community in Dej was destroyed, and besides, the few Jews who had survived the war didn't want to live among people who had betrayed them. I certainly had no desire to stay in Dej. Everyone I had loved who had lived there was dead. We needed to find the fastest way possible to Israel.

We discovered that wasn't at all easy. Israel — then called Palestine — wasn't an independent country as it is today. It was a chunk of the Middle East that the British took from the Ottoman Empire after the end of the First World War. From 1920 on the British established what they called "Mandatory Palestine." The land may have been inhabited by Arabs and Jews, but in effect, the Brits ran the place and did whatever they could to limit immigration there. Sneaking into Palestine was extremely risky, and needless to say, the Arabs didn't want us in there either.

So we had to be practical. For us three brothers, that meant first moving to Italy, where we had heard there were some functioning Jewish "transit camps" that could assist us with our immigration plans. We made the nearly 1,500-kilometre journey from Dej to Milan, Italy, assisted by an organization whose mission it was to help Holocaust survivors. Each family had its own room at these transit camps, so I shared a room with Shuli, while Dudi and Olga had their own room.

It was 1946, and not only were we very focused on getting to Israel, but we also had committed ourselves to the Zionist dream of recreating a homeland for the Jews in an independent state. Much of the world was either indifferent to that Zionist dream or actively against it. But some favoured the creation of a state, in part because of the Jewish people's historic claim to and ongoing presence in the land, but also, no doubt, out of a collective sense of guilt, given the horrific treatment Jews had just undergone at the hands of the Nazis.

So Shuli secretly joined an organization called the Irgun, a Zionist paramilitary group, whose goal was to liberate the land of Israel and help establish an independent Jewish state. Its full name in Hebrew was "Ha-Irgun Ha-Tzvai Ha-Leumi be-Eretz Yisrael" (The National Military Organization in the Land of Israel). The Irgun was an offshoot of another Jewish paramilitary organization called the Haganah, which is the Hebrew word for "defence." But the Irgun was considered more radical than the Haganah. It took its mission from the teachings of the Russian-born author, poet, orator, and soldier Vladimir Jabotinsky, who believed, as American historian Howard Sachar described it: "Every Jew had the right to enter Palestine; only active retaliation would deter the Arabs; only Jewish armed force would ensure the Jewish state."

It was also in Italy that Dudi married his girlfriend Olga. We all settled in a refugee camp near Milan in northern Italy called Scuola Cadorna. Soon enough, Dudi and Olga had a newborn baby daughter and took an apartment in the camp. They named the daughter Sara, after our sister who was murdered in Auschwitz. And incidentally, that would be the last time Dudi would ever reference the Holocaust in our presence. He henceforth refused to discuss any details of his connection to this time in history.

Soon, I separated from my brothers and got transferred from Milan to a refugee camp near Rome, run by the Betar Movement. Betar was a Zionist youth movement, again, established by Jabotinsky (who, when he moved to Israel, changed his name to something less Russian and more Israeli sounding — Ze'ev Jabotinsky). The reason for my transfer was simple — education. I needed to go to school and make up for my lost years.

I spent a year and half in Italy, and it was a wonderful time. The people were kind to the Jews. In fact, Italy didn't have a centuries-long problem with anti-Semitism. Even Benito Mussolini said in 1932: "Anti-Semitism doesn't exist in Italy. Italians of Jewish birth have shown themselves good citizens, and they fought bravely in the war. Many of them occupy leading positions in the universities, in the army, in the banks." Of course, that was before Mussolini embraced his part in the Final Solution, trying to ingratiate himself with Hitler. However, it's also worth noting that Italians saved thousands of Jews from extermination camps by hiding them in their homes and helping them escape to safe places. Maybe it's because the Jews and

Italians are quite simpatico. When I lived there, I learned the language and communicated with Italians without difficulty.

I also think Italians and Jews got along so well in Italy because many Italians felt considerable personal guilt at the treatment of their country's Jewish community. It was as if much of the country collectively bought into the madness of Hitler's Final Solution. But then in the dying days of the war, Italians captured and killed Mussolini, then hung him upside down on meat hooks from the roof of a gas station. It seemed after the war, Italy wanted re-entry into the family of civilized nations.

In any event, there was a heartwarming meeting in Milan that deeply touched me and showed me that people could really understand our situation and were willing to help in every way they could. One day, my brothers and I went to the city to shop. The problem was that I didn't have any clothes, except for what was on my back and the prison camp uniform from Mauthausen, which I kept in my closet back home. We went to one of the biggest stores in Milan to find a nice suit, and a couple of shirts. As we were looking around, someone approached me and asked: "Te vagy az, Moritz?" (Is that you, Moritz?). He was an older man, in his thirties, and I didn't recognize him at all. But I confirmed that he was right, my concentration camp name was Moritz.

Then the man continued: "Nem emlékszel rám? Gunskirchen blokk száma hét?" (Don't you remember me? Gunskirchen, Block Number Seven?).

Suddenly, it all came back to me. I remembered him. He was, indeed, a man from my block, a Spaniard who was a political prisoner. Perhaps he was one of those communists who left Spain after the civil war and ended up in a German camp.

Political prisoners in Nazi camps were treated better than Jews and certainly had a better chance to survive. And now, here he was, in Milan, owning this huge store.

"Mit keres Moritz?" (What are you looking for Moritz?) he asked me.

"Szükségem van valami szépet a kopás miatt tervezi, hogy térjen át az izraeli vagyok" (I need something nice to wear because I'm planning to move to Israel), I said.

My friend told me to get a suitcase as big as I wanted and fill it up with anything I liked — all on the house. What a generous offer.

We talked a little bit more (in Italian, I think) and reminisced about the camp and our friends there. He told me he supported my decision to go to Israel. We could only talk for another ten or fifteen minutes — I just couldn't go on, it was too painful. The memories were too fresh. My brothers agreed. They urged me to stop talking about it as well.

I didn't abuse my friend's kindness but did manage to leave the store with a couple of nice suits and several shirts — the first nice clothes I had owned in a long time. Strangely enough, I can't remember the man's name, but his kindness was unforgettable.

In my Italian school, I learned a little of bit Hebrew, studied math, and some other general subjects. The teachers came from Israel. One of the teachers was a man in his early thirties named Yechiel Kadishai. He taught us Hebrew and many important facts about Israel: the current situation there, and plans for independence and sovereignty. I would meet up with Kadishai many years later, under most extraordinary circumstances, but I won't spoil that story by telling it here.

I remained in boarding school for about six months. There were many such schools across Europe, all funded by the American Jewish Joint Distribution Committee, nicknamed "The Joint," a worldwide Jewish relief organization. The schools weren't exclusively for Holocaust survivors. There were also young people from Russia and other places affected by the war. I was a little older than the average student, so I was appointed a youth leader. Beyond academics, we learned some basic military discipline and marched "left, right, left right."

As we prepared to make *aliyah* (a move to Israel), the teachers talked in detail about political life there, the national leaders, the different political parties and movements. We discussed the various manifestos and argued ourselves hoarse debating which political parties served Israel's future best.

I've already told you that my brother Shuli joined the Irgun. Now, someone from the school contacted me and asked if I wanted to join the underground organization as well.

Did I want to join? Of course I did! It was my dream. I had discussed it with my brothers many times. I very much wanted to fight for Israeli independence, even though I was just a teenager.

Being part of the Irgun also meant swearing an oath of secrecy. Clearly my brother Shuli had done so. At that time, he had still not yet informed me that he was in the Irgun. The organization worked in cells of five people. The point was, if a member were ever captured, he wouldn't be able to pass along too much information to his captors.

I was next relocated to another camp in northern Italy called Arona, where we started more intense military training, practising with arms and ammunition. This was all done in secret. The Italian authorities merely assumed we were studying science, the humanities, and other subjects usually taught in school. We took physics and chemistry in our school, but mostly to improve our skill in handling explosives and guns. If any Italian officials understood the real purpose of our efforts, a little bribery here and there usually took care of their curiosity.

We followed events in Palestine very closely and prepared for a time when we would be useful to the Israeli independence movement. I got more skilled in handling weapons and could dismantle a gun with my eyes closed. We also carried out some dangerous operations involving significant risk. Once, I was part of a group whose mission was to steal a cache of weapons from British troops, headquartered at a hotel. I didn't actually enter the building, but stayed on watch outside, then helped load the Tommy guns into the truck. Had we been caught, the Brits would not have been amused. Prison would have awaited us, or worse.

After several months of training, we were told that a ship with 153 million Francs worth of military armaments donated to Israel by the French government was on its way to Italy. It was called the *Altalena*, named after a pseudonym for Jabotinsky. The *Altalena* had left Marseille on the south shore of France, and was moving towards Italy to pick us up. We would then see the ship through to its eventual destination: Israel, which declared its independence only a few weeks earlier, on May 14, 1948.

There was, however, one catch — only bachelors could participate on this mission. It was too dangerous to risk a family man, which meant that Dudi, now happily married and with a baby daughter on his hands, would have to stay.

A week before we were to board this arms smuggling ship, I met with Shuli and only then did we discover that we were both Irgun members. He was completely surprised at my revelation but happy to have me on the mission. Other groups would join us from Germany and Czechoslovakia (which in those days was still one country — it didn't split into the Czech Republic and Slovakia until 1993).

The ship finally arrived in early June 1948. We were all armed. I had a handgun and got assigned to a group responsible for security on the ship. We were allowed to take very few personal belongings on board, as there was no extra space. The ship was jam-packed with weapons and ammunition. I did take my new suits that my Spanish friend gave me in Milan. I also took my concentration camp uniform from Mauthausen with me. Truthfully, I have no earthly idea why I continued to keep that reminder of what I had endured. I certainly had no desire to try to remember that chapter of my life. In fact, quite the contrary: I wanted to forget it all. So why keep this uniform? I didn't have a good answer back then, and I don't have one now. Perhaps I was subconsciously thinking: for anyone who might try to deny my experience, who disbelieve what I've been through, well, here's your proof that it really happened. Maybe. So I saved my hat, my coat, my shirt, and a knife as proof of my torment and brought it with me on to the *Altalena*.

If we had any illusions about the dangerousness of the mission we had signed up for, we were immediately disabused of that. Our commanders told us to be prepared for anything, even death. No one was making any promises that we'd arrive in Israel alive. The Mediterranean Sea was full of dangers. There were Arab ships desperately trying to prevent any help from the outside world getting to the newly created state of Israel. We knew if we were discovered, we'd be sunk without delay. The British ships would likely do the same because they had orders to stop any arms deliveries to the Israeli troops. Israel may have declared independence, but international recognition of that fact in the United Nations was still a year away. Our orders were simple: get those weapons to Israel, and help the Irgun play its role in securing Israel's future. Failure wasn't an option. If we were ordered by foreign powers to turn over our weapons cache, we would refuse to obey. We would fight, and almost certainly die in an effort to complete our mission. But I didn't care. My father's words were constantly on my mind: "Go to Israel. We will meet again in Israel."

The British ships really concerned us because they were equipped with modern radar. If they saw us on their screens, we were finished. We monitored the sea around the clock and I was in the watch group. We hardly ever slept. We had standing orders to fire on any suspicious attackers. Any ship on the horizon could be an enemy. Even what looked like a fishing boat could in fact be an Arab vessel armed with cannon and machine guns. We carefully changed course every time there was something suspicious in the view.

Our journey took us about a week. Several times during the trip, the crew was put on red alert. Each time, however, it was just a training drill. We were lucky and made it through the entire voyage unnoticed.

We arrived near the shores of Tel Aviv on June 20, 1948. What a feeling it was! I was overcome with emotions and couldn't hold back the tears. I thought of my lost family — my two sisters, and my parents. They all wanted to come here one day. Since childhood, it had been a dream for many in the Jewish community of Dej. Like all Jewish families around the globe, we concluded every Passover Seder, with the words: "Next year in Jerusalem." While many people who say it may not truly mean it, we did. And now my dream was finally coming true. Israel would be my new home, offering a new life, replacing the one I had lost. I continued to cry at the thought of my father's words, that we would meet again in Israel. His body was long gone, but I knew his soul was here watching over me.

What I didn't know at the time was that the *Altalena* would soon become massively embroiled in internal Israeli politics. Israel's first prime minister, David Ben Gurion, was trying to absorb all the external paramilitary organizations, including the Irgun, into a new Israel Defense Forces (IDF), to protect the new country from a multi-front invasion by several neighbouring Arab countries. As part of that effort, the Irgun was supposed to commit to ending its own private arms acquisitions. And yet, here we were with nearly 1,000 fighters on board a ship teeming with weapons, including 5,000 rifles, 250 Bren guns, 5 million bullets, and 50 bazookas.

But there was more. On June 11, 1948, a ceasefire was negotiated between Israel and its Arab neighbours, a ceasefire which prohibited either side from bringing in more weapons from outside sources. So the Irgun leader in Israel, Menachem Begin (yes, the same Begin who would become prime minister), cleverly postponed the ship's arrival, and undertook to negotiate with Ben Gurion as to what should happen next.

What we didn't know was that neither the Arabs nor the British were our prime concerns now. The Ben Gurion provisional government of Israel was. Begin wanted to ensure that a healthy percentage of the weaponry ended up in the hands of Irgun fighters, so those fighters could liberate Jerusalem. Ben Gurion had already agreed to that arrangement, but at this moment seemed more concerned about ensuring the smooth absorption of the Irgun into the IDF. So he unilaterally broke his pact with Begin. He didn't want an army within an army. He also wanted to demonstrate his unrivalled political power within Israeli politics, and Begin stood in the way of that.

In fact, in discussions with his colleagues, Ben Gurion suggested that the need to ensure that his forces controlled all the weaponry was so essential that he would order his troops to open fire on the *Altalena* to make it so.

What did we on the ship expect? Naturally, we were expecting a hero's welcome! Having recently survived the Holocaust, we now successfully risked our necks to bring the *Altalena* to Israel. "I'm coming home, *Tateh*. I'm coming home," I kept whispering to myself. The concentration camps would be a memory. "Everything will be different now."

We had bypassed the port of Tel Aviv (negotiations between Ben Gurion and Begin saw to that — they figured the ship would attract too much attention from international observers there) and landed in a harbour near Kfar Vitkin, about forty kilometres north. To show you how out of touch we were with the political realities of the day, all of us on board were singing and hugging — that's how joyous we were at what we thought was the successful conclusion of our mission. We were looking forward to unloading our cargo, then starting the rest of our lives building our new country. We could see a long line of buses waiting on the shore, presumably to take us to our new homes and jobs.

Our crew started unloading the weapons. But as they did so, they were informed by Ben Gurion's representatives that all the weapons were to be surrendered to their authority. An original deal, which would have allowed the Irgun to keep a percentage of the weapons, was apparently unilaterally cancelled by Ben Gurion, who mistrusted Begin's motives, even though he was a loyal Zionist merely trying to help his country. I mistrusted the Ben Gurion faction's motives and thought they were trying to consolidate their power.

Frankly, I was disgusted and dismayed with the whole thing. We had no problem sharing our cache with the IDF. But to turn everything over? Hell, no!

Again, what we didn't know was that our hero and leader Menachem Begin was essentially threatened by Ben Gurion's government — give us the weapons, or else. Here's some of the ultimatum that was sent to Begin:

To: M. Begin

By special order from the Chief of the General Staff of the Israel Defense Forces, I am empowered to confiscate the weapons and military materials which have arrived on the Israeli coast in the area of my jurisdiction in the name of the Israel Government. I have been authorized to demand that you hand over the weapons to me

for safekeeping.... You are required to carry out
this order immediately. If you do not agree ... I
shall use all the means at my disposal in order
to implement the order and to requisition the
weapons which have reached shore and transfer
them from private possession into the possession of the Israel government.... The entire area
is surrounded by fully armed military units and
armored cars, and all roads are blocked. I hold
you fully responsible for any consequences in
the event of your refusal to carry out this order.
The immigrants — unarmed — will be permitted to travel to the camps in accordance with your
arrangements. You have ten minutes to give me
your answer.

— D.E.,

Brigade Commander

When we got wind of this disagreement and Ben Gurion's
breaking his word to Begin, our people stopped unloading the
weapons. In turn, that angered those on shore who insisted the
orders of the higher command of the Israeli army had to be
obeyed. But our soldiers had our own orders. We stayed put.

Harsh words were exchanged, and feelings ran high. Finally,
a fight broke out. At first, it was just pushing and shoving, but
it quickly turned into full-fledged hits and blows. I was still on
the ship's deck in my security role, completely unaware of what
was transpiring. My brother and I certainly saw that something
was amiss, but since it never occurred to us that Jews would be

fighting with Jews, we assumed that it was the Arabs who were trying to prevent us from unloading our guns.

Meanwhile, the political machinations got more complicated. Begin, who was now on shore, refused to respond to the ultimatum. He drove to nearby Netanya to confer with his colleagues, then returned to the beach to confer with his officers. Suddenly, a firefight broke out. I couldn't tell you which side shot first, but in the midst of it all, Begin bravely took a rowboat to the *Altalena*, which itself was now under attack by corvettes offshore. On shore, Irgun fighters were overrun and surrendered.

This was all just crazy! Israel desperately needed the weapons we were delivering. Moreover, Ben Gurion was breaking his original agreement allowing the Irgun to keep some of the weapons for its own Jerusalem Battalion, which was trying to fight and win the war of independence.

Once Begin arrived on the *Altalena*, he ordered the ship to head south for Tel Aviv, where the Irgun had a stronger base of support. It was a defiant move, no question about it, and it prompted rumours that Begin might mount a coup against Ben Gurion's provisional government. But did it make sense to stay at Kfar Vitkin? Once the shooting had broken out, six Irgun soldiers were killed with eighteen more wounded. Two IDF soldiers were also dead, with six more wounded. Jews killing Jews? Even worse, Jews killing Jewish survivors of the Holocaust? After all we had been through? Impossible. Except it wasn't.

Of course, those of us on board had no clue about any of this. What we also didn't know was that Ben Gurion allegedly gave the order to fire cannons and sink the *Altalena*, despite the fact that nearly a thousand of us were still on board. As Shlomo

Nakdimon's reports in his book, *Altalena*, three pilots refused fire, saying: "You can kiss my foot. I did not lose four friends and fly 10,000 miles in order to bomb Jews." We did, however, sustain fire from the corvettes that were tracking us to Tel Aviv. The following day, after arriving at the Tel Aviv harbour, Ben Gurion gave the order to begin shelling the *Altalena*. Again, some soldiers refused. One said he was willing to be executed for his insubordination and that it would constitute "the best thing I ever did with my life." Another said he "didn't come to the land of Israel to fight against Jews."

Menachem Begin was now on the ship as well and I suspect he was shocked that it had come to this. It was on that morning, June 22, 1948, that I got my first opportunity to see this amazing man and exceptional political leader close up. There was nothing special about him on the surface. He looked like just another average-looking man in his mid-thirties (in fact, he was thirty-four). But to us, he was already a hero. He was the leader of the Irgun, which had fought so heroically to liberate Israel.

It was a sunny summer day when we stopped near the beaches of Tel Aviv. The people in the city had heard the news that the ship was coming and there were crowds all along the coastline. While we were busy preparing to unload our cargo for a second time, that's when the shelling started again. Several IDF shells hit the water around the vessel. They were allegedly warning shots. Then, suddenly, one shell hit the boat and caused a massive explosion. There was smoke everywhere, and men were screaming their lungs out. Many of our ranks surrounded Begin, presumably to create a human shield and protect him in case the IDF tried to kill him. We genuinely feared he would be the target of an assassination attempt. That would certainly have solved one of Ben Gurion's political problems. (Ben Gurion represented Mapai, an acronym for the Workers Party in the Land of Israel, which became part of the Labour government. Begin, conversely, founded the conservative Likud coalition.)

Through no particular skill or genius of my own, I found myself at a pivotal moment in Israeli history. The stakes were simply incalculable. My shipmates and I had ample firepower at our disposal. We probably had enough weaponry to defeat our IDF adversaries on shore. But at what cost? What would have been the consequences of returning fire? Could we have started a civil war only one month after Israel's founding? Could the break between Ben Gurion and Begin have permanently divided our society? I know this: Menachem Begin never feared fighting. He had proven it on numerous occasions in the past. And I know he was prepared for one more fight at that moment, as he stood on the deck of the *Altalena* with a pistol in his hands.

But what did Begin do? In my view, he saved the country. He put whatever personal ambitions and misgivings he had about Ben Gurion aside, and did what a real leader does when the common interest is at stake. He ordered us not to shoot back. He took out his pistol and said: "We are not going to have a civil war here." He added that he would personally gun down anyone who disobeyed his orders. Then he ordered us to leave the ship.

It was still a chaotic scene. The shooting continued and more bombs fell near the boat. Many of us feared the ammunition we were carrying on board would explode because of the fire on the ship, and so my brother Shuli and I jumped overboard into the water. Many others followed. And still, the IDF soldiers from the shore continued to strafe the water, shooting at us. Another shell then hit the ship, prompting more screams, more wounded, and more killed. I remember that one of the dead was a Holocaust survivor. He had endured terrible ordeals in the camps, and yet he died when he got to Israel. He came to Italy from Czechoslovakia, and during the preparations for the expedition, was one of those in charge of collecting arms. We met and became friends on the ship, and talked about our past lives and plans for the future. His name was Israel Akiva. He survived the Nazis, but not his fellow Israelis. What an outrage to have Jewish soldiers firing at Jewish Holocaust survivors as our ship was sinking. It truly was an insane situation.

When Shuli and I swam to shore, we were apprehended and taken into custody at gunpoint by IDF troopers. We were soaking wet, shocked, and deeply frustrated with the turn of events. It was as if we were once again in a German concentration camp, surrounded by guards who would shoot if we made an attempt to escape. I couldn't believe Jews could point weapons at other Jews.

It's hard to convey our feelings of despair. We came to Israel with passion and hopes for realizing a lifelong dream. It was that dream that had helped my brother and I survive the death camps. We always considered Israel our homeland too. Instead, our compatriots greeted us with bullets and bombs. Sixteen of our people on the *Altalena* were killed. We were in shock, as if the world had suddenly turned topsy-turvy on us. And there we stood, wet, frustrated, and powerless like prisoners of war, with somber-faced troops escorting us, their guns pointed at our chests.

I turned to Shuli and told him: "Let's go back. Back to Italy. I don't want to stay here." And then something amazing happened that changed the course of my life. One of the soldiers who had been staring at my brother for quite some time suddenly screamed: "Oh, my God! Are you Shuli Markovits? What is this? What is happening? Why I am doing this? Why I am holding my gun to you?" He was from our hometown of Dej and he recognized Shuli. With tears in his eyes he literally tossed his gun away and joined us. Then some other troopers in our escort began chatting with us, asking who we were, how we got on this ship, and so on. Perhaps, I thought, we were not among enemies after all.

The now much-friendlier soldiers took us to some military quarters where we were able to change our clothes and put on something dry.

By now, I knew enough Hebrew to catch snatches of conversations and heard that the *Altalena* had been set ablaze and sunk by the IDF. I also heard that Menachem Begin was deeply disappointed and was seen crying. It was a terrible tragedy for him too, even though many years later he described his decision not to start an Israeli civil war as the greatest accomplishment of his life.

The image of Menachem Begin on that ship, acting in the responsible way he did, has stayed deeply imprinted in my memory. I became convinced that Begin was a man of integrity, someone who could really lead the nation, and never mind what his opponents thought of him. Even as a mere boy of sixteen years of age, I felt I had an intuition about people's true nature. I just thought Begin had the royal jelly mixed with true integrity and that I got a glimpse of it in June 1948 on the *Altalena*.

Elka Harnik Markovits, Mordechai's mother. The only artifact Mordechai has of his life before the war.

Mordechai with his brothers after the Second World War, 1945. Back row from left to right: family friend, Olga Rozencweig, Dudi Rozencweig, Shalom Markovits. Front row: Mordechai Ronen.

The *Altalena* on the shores of Tel Aviv, June 1948.

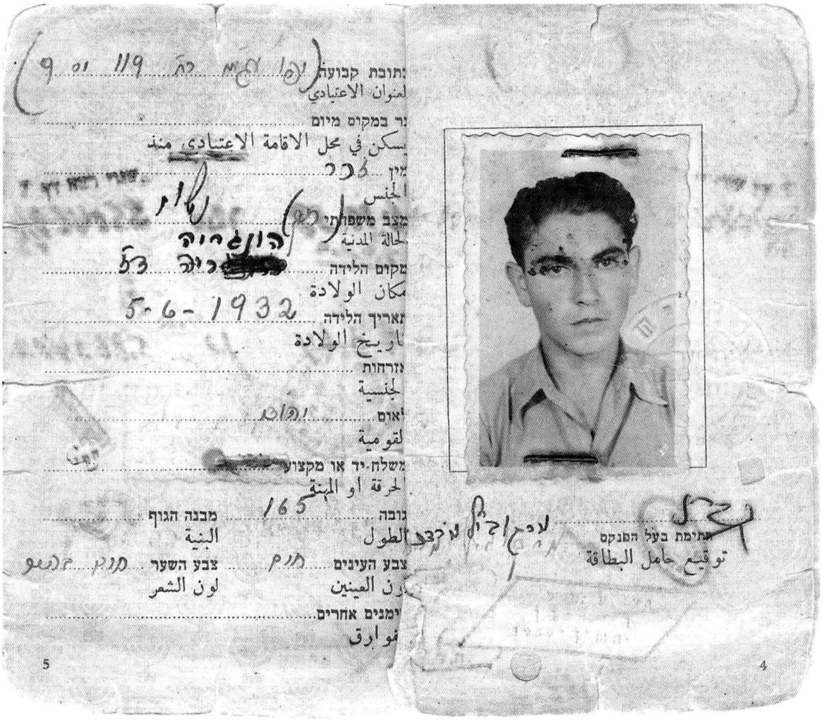


Mordechai’s first Israeli identification card, 1948.

Mordechai, the IDF soldier, stands at attention, early 1950s.

Mordechai (far right) and his brother Shalom (third from right) singing in a synagogue choir in Israel, mid-1950s.

The wedding of Mordechai and Ilana Ronen, March 17, 1958.

Mordechai and his brothers. From left to right: Dudi Rozencweig, Shalom Markovits, Mordechai Ronen, mid-1980s.

Mordechai marking a grave for his murdered family members during his first return visit to Auschwitz, April 1992. (Photo by Steve Paikin.)

Mordechai is overcome with emotion as he walks through Auschwitz I with Canadian prime minister Jean Chrétien, January 1999. From left to right: Mordechai's son, Moshe; Mordechai; Jean Chrétien; Aline Chrétien. (Photo by Jean-Marc Carisse.)

Sixty-seven years later, I still hold the same opinion of that man. I know that many people disagree with me. Begin still remains a controversial figure in Israeli history. Some believe that he was a terrorist, pointing to the King David Hotel bombing in Jerusalem in July 1946 as evidence. At that time, the hotel was the site of the headquarters of the British Mandatory authorities of Palestine. An attack was conducted in an attempt to force British authorities to leave the territory and give independence to the Jewish state. The explosion resulted in terrible casualties: ninety-one people of various nationalities died and forty-six more were wounded. Since Begin was the head of the Irgun, the responsibility for this attack was placed on him. Begin always said he gave the British half an hour's notice of the attack, and I believe him. For some reason, the Brits chose not to evacuate the hotel. Maybe it was their arrogance. Begin always contended the British declined to evacuate the hotel so they could vilify his paramilitary group afterwards. Whatever the explanation, I believe that Begin did give the British adequate notice to evacuate. Why? For the same reason he didn't allow bloodshed during the *Altalena* incident — he was a tough leader, but he wasn't a cold-blooded, cynical killer who would do anything to achieve his goals.

Almost three decade after the *Altalena* episode, on May 17, 1977, Israelis elected Menachem Begin as their prime minister. Most observers thought it would never happen — that he'd never amount to anything other than a cranky opposition leader. They were wrong. I can recall getting together with friends of mine in Toronto at the time he was elected and they were all certain that Begin's election meant immediate war with the Arabs. Begin's bellicosity was well known. But I had my doubts. "I'm not sure," I said. "Maybe there will be war, but maybe not." Sure enough, a little over a year after becoming prime minister, Begin put his signature on the longest-lasting peace agreement the Middle East has ever seen — the Camp David Accords with Egypt. That was the Begin I knew and loved from the *Altalena*.

I suppose I should mention one more postscript in the *Altalena* story. When the ship sank to the bottom of the Mediterranean, it also took with it a suitcase of mine. The suitcase contained the beautiful, fine clothes my friend from Spain had given me as a gift. They were now gone, along with my prisoner uniform from Mauthausen that included my hat, coat, shirt, and knife, which I had kept for inexplicable reasons for four years. To this day, those reminders of the most gruesome chapter of my life remain at the bottom of the ocean.

Maybe it's for the best.

# 7

# From Markovits to Ronen

Thanks to the more positive experience with Israel Defense
Forces soldiers in the aftermath of the *Altalena* incident, and
due to some lobbying by my brother Shuli, the decision was
made: we were going to stay in Israel and make our new lives
there. Also, if we wanted to stay close together as a family,
there really was no other choice. And so, with that, Mordechai
Markovits became a private in the IDF at age sixteen.

My first task was to figure out where to stay. I didn't have
a cent to my name, so the first place where I thought I could
find shelter was the Irgun headquarters on King George Street
in Tel Aviv called Metzudat Ze'ev (it translates to "Ze'ev's
Fortress," a reference to Jabotinsky). As a former member of
the unit, I assumed I could get some help there. In fact, there
were many former soldiers there, needing a bed and breakfast,
and some of us were veterans from the *Altalena*. During the

day, we would fan out around the city, doing whatever jobs we could find. But in the evening we former *Altalena* crewmembers often regrouped in an Irgun club located near our shelter. There we could socialize in the warm atmosphere of our fellow brothers, make new friends, and gather information about job vacancies or other possibilities. We'd stay late into the night, entertaining ourselves as well with lots of singing.

I have to confess that I don't recall Israelis themselves being particularly helpful to me. But there was one significant exception to this trend. Once again, the details of how this came together escape me, but somehow, I became acquainted with a wonderful Yemenite family who started asking questions about how I came to be in Israel, and what were my plans now. After a little small talk, the family invited Shuli and me to consider them part of our extended family until we could get our lives better organized.

This family's generosity stood in stark contrast to the treatment I received from most Israelis, who, frankly, weren't that friendly at all. In the meantime, rumours continued to spread about the *Altalena* incident, much of it complete fabrication, but it added to many people's sense of unease about me.

The fact is, we were different from some of the Israelis who were already living in the Holy Land. We were Ashkenazi Jews whose lineage went back to eastern Europe. Our first language was Yiddish, not Hebrew. Our traditions, particularly compared to Sephardic Jews, were quite different, adding to the distrust some people had for us.

The Yemenite family, however, appeared not to be burdened by these feelings. They seemed to understand our situation better than most, perhaps because they were newcomers to Israel as well. They had also gone through a period of adaptation after emigrating from Yemen. They were just very kind people who felt it was their duty to help others get through hard times. We frequently visited and had meals with them. I remember in the mornings, we had fresh bread with honey for breakfast. This seemed a luxury from another lifetime. The Yemenites gave us some clothes and helped in every way they could. I had to conclude that perhaps my expectations for our new lives in Israel were too high at first. But now, we felt love from a warm, family environment. It was wonderful. Remember, I was just sixteen. It had been too many years since we had lived in anything remotely close to a normal family situation. But we experienced it with that family, and I will always be grateful for that.

Our next task was to become real soldiers in the IDF. From our recruitment centre, we were sent to Northern Galilee to join the army fighting against Arab troops. Despite my training in Italy, I still had a lot to learn about becoming a real uniformed soldier. I was unfamiliar with the weapons the IDF used. Fortunately, the authorities agreed to allow my brother and me to be assigned to the same unit. Shuli had a much more extensive knowledge of firearms and he showed me how to handle these different rifles.

We sat in trenches and occasionally exchanged fire with the enemy. Most days were relatively quiet, but, as seems to be my custom, there was yet another brush with death. Sometimes when it was dark, the Arab soldiers would try to crawl close to our positions and throw grenades in our trenches. They rarely succeeded in doing so, but on one occasion, near the Syrian border, one of them managed to do it. The grenade landed directly in front of me, just a few feet away. I assumed this was it. There simply wasn't enough time to react and escape from my predicament. I couldn't take my eyes off the grenade, waiting for it to explode and kill me, my brother, and other soldiers next to us. The situation was surreal. The seconds dragged on. All of us were just mesmerized, staring at this bomb, and then … nothing. For some reason, the grenade didn't explode. Quickly, Shuli leaped towards it, grabbed it, and threw it out of our trench. And then it exploded! I have no explanation for our good fortune. I only knew that someone or something seemed to be watching over me again.

The attacks and bombings actually never stopped after that, and some in our group were killed. One day I did sustain some kind of leg wound — nothing serious — just a scratch from a stray bullet or some shrapnel, I don't even remember anymore. Nevertheless, it did require treatment at a hospital in Safed (pronounced Tzfat), a city in the north of Israel.

It was in this hospital that I was told that my military career was over. I was going to be released from military service because I wasn't even supposed to be in the army in the first place. Being sixteen, I was considered too young. I couldn't quite figure out how they knew I was that young. After all, I'd been lying about my age for years, making sure my Israeli documents reflected what I'd done ever since I got to Auschwitz — adding a couple of years to my age to save my life. Now it was simply a habit I didn't even think about.

I guess the truth was, I wasn't very tall, and really didn't look eighteen. The officer in charge of my unit simply asked me directly if I was lying about my age. He was a good and kind man and I just couldn't lie to him, so I told him the truth. He smiled and told me that it would be in my own best interest if I left the army. There were age requirements, and I needed two more years to be able to serve legally. I could see that the officer's concern for me was sincere, and I also knew it was time to stop misleading the people around me. I was in a different world, surrounded by friends, not enemies. Perhaps, I thought, it was time to get a normal job, then I could revisit the idea of joining the military in a couple of years. I also knew this meant leaving Shuli, since he wanted to stay in the army. We spent two final weeks together at a military clinic (Shuli was also receiving treatment for a small injury) and then we parted ways. My brother went back to the front lines, while I moved to Tel Aviv, ready to begin civilian life.

The Irgun club continued to be my most important home base, and for reasons more than simple companionship. There was another member of the club who showed up frequently, whose company I thoroughly enjoyed — Menachem Begin. Our encounters allowed me to really get to know Begin personally. We all wanted to hear from Begin, and ask him questions. He was one of those magnetic personalities who attracted a crowd wherever he went. I would also often go to hear Begin speak in public, where I thought he was the most passionate, mesmerizing speaker I'd ever heard. But he was also very approachable and liked to participate in all kinds of activities in the club, including singing. One of the soldiers from the ship wrote lyrics to the music my brother Shuli wrote about the *Altalena*, and it became something of an anthem for us crew members. Begin heard me perform the song and loved it so much that we often sang it together thereafter. Because I usually led the song, he got interested in me and wanted to know more about me. Of course, he didn't remember my face from the *Altalena,* but we often talked about life and family, and he offered his support for my intention to become an army officer in the future.

My singing helped me in a more practical way too. Without sounding like I'm boasting, people in the club just loved me! To them, I was the cute kid with the nice voice. I became popular and the more people learned of my life story, the more they wanted to help me. One time, there was a young Yiddish-speaking girl, just a little older than me, who invited me to her home because she thought her father could get me a job. The man turned out to be nice and connected. He introduced me to some other people, and eventually I got a job working at an ammunition factory.

Life in Israel was looking up. During the day I worked at the factory, and in the evening I usually went to the Irgun club and sang the *Altalena* song. Here it is translated into English:

> We set out on a journey,
> To fight and suffer for thee,
> Bringing with us the spirit of battle,
> And a ship loaded with arms to set you free.

> And if you are wondering from where,
> We got all this ammunition,
> Then you will understand Caine,
> That Ezel will live on forever.

> For many long years in Europe we waited,
> We struggled for you without end,
> And the results of that labour, *Altalena*,
> Was for you, our country, our homeland.

And the way you received us,
God, we will never forget!
We dreamt of our soldier brothers,
But were confronted by the fire of cannons.

Although the *Altalena* was sunk,
Soldiers, raise your heads high with pride,
To the whole land of Israel,
We will stay loyal forever!

It was a challenging time for Israel. Most of the country was poor. Everyone had to work extremely hard to build the country, but there was a general feeling of enthusiasm about finally becoming an independent nation. The one thing I wish I could have done was get more formal education, but there were no scholarships available. The country simply had other priorities. So I worked hard at the factory and made enough money to support myself with a little extra for entertainment. I was even able to afford a real luxury item — a bicycle. Having a bike was actually quite a rare thing in those days. But at the same time, having that bike gave me a constant headache. There were other kids around, and you wouldn't believe how jealous they were of my having a bicycle — not just boys, but adults too. At that time, buying a car was out of the question for practically anyone so a bike was on the top of everyone's list of desires. So I had to watch that bike around the clock lest anyone steal it. It was my Cadillac.

One day, my employment at the factory suddenly ended. Though I worked hard, the administration fired me without any explanation, although I had my suspicions as to why they terminated me. My guess was, they heard about my involvement with the *Altalena*, which somehow tarnished me in their eyes and made me unreliable.

In any event, it was 1950 and I found myself unemployed, without a completed education or an experienced profession to fall back on — with one exception: I was a soldier.

I was eighteen — legal for the IDF — and the combination of needing a job and wanting to help protect my new country from its rather unfriendly neighbours made the decision easy.

As I joined the army, I made another decision that many new Israelis make. I decided to change my family name. I left Markovits behind me and took on a new last name: Ronen. Ronen means singing for joy or gladness. It made so much sense for me because our family in Dej always joyously sang our lungs out. I actually first heard the name from one of my teachers, a young woman, who must have heard me sing and suggested it. "You might not like it, but just think about it, because it is you," she told me. I instantly agreed. It felt right, almost as if I had been born with the name. Mordechai Markovits was no more. I was now Mordechai Ronen. (Later, in the army, my friends starting calling me by my nickname "Motke"; neither of my two brothers changed their names.)

I went to an army recruitment center in Tel Aviv, and once again my experience with the *Altalena* followed me. Except this time there was no room for interpretation or ambiguity, as there was with my previous munitions job. One of the officials at the centre tried to give me his best advice when he heard that I arrived in Israel aboard the *Altalena*.

"Be reasonable," he told me. "If you include that, it will hurt your future and maybe even ruin your career." You have to understand: the Israeli government was in the hands of the Labour Party. Menachem Begin, who became a member of the Knesset (the Israeli Parliament) in 1949, was the main opposition to the government. The army official wasn't threatening me. He was just telling me to be politically smart and to lie. If you wanted to get ahead at that time, reminding everyone that you were aligned with the leader of the opposition wasn't smart.

But I wasn't going to play along. I admired Begin and had no hesitation saying so. "No," I told the official, "I'm going to tell the truth. I have nothing to be ashamed of."

He came back at me one more time. "Do you understand that people will discriminate against you for exactly that reason?" he asked.

"Yes, I do," I replied. And that was that. I could not betray my affection for Begin or my commitment to that mission. I may only have been eighteen years old, but I was fully aware of the consequences of my decision. I also knew there were some things in life that were more important and valuable than moving up the ranks.

So I showed up to Camp Tzrifin in central Israel, preparing to take my licks as the new kid on the block. However, much to my surprise, they appointed me to train others. I guess I assumed my *Altalena* connection would hold me back. Instead, I was actually something of a veteran compared to everyone else. Again, remember that Israel, as a country, was less than two years old at that point. Everything was new and had to be built from scratch: a political system, its economy, education system, and armed forces. So my three months of basic training in Italy, plus my short time in the trenches during the War of Independence, made me one of the more experienced hands. I certainly didn't feel that way. In fact, one episode during that war made me feel quite stupid.

I was such a rookie (and so was my brother Shuli ) that when we threw grenades at the enemy, we neglected to take out the pins so those grenades could explode. We threw them as if they were rocks. I'm sure we bonked a few enemy troops on the head, but in hindsight that wasn't exactly protocol for trying to take out the enemy. We had a good laugh about it when we finally figured out how to use the grenades properly. But I wondered after rejoining the army if I was really experienced enough to train others. Then I realized, the soldiers I was supposed to train had probably never even seen a grenade before, let alone thrown one. Having said that, not all our new recruits were babes in the woods. There were some who had fought against the Nazis. For example, two of my trainees included a former British general and a former Red Army colonel — both highly skilled military career men, from whom I learned a lot about the art of war. But, of course, we all needed to integrate into a new country's army, with new ways, and new warfare challenges.

After a few months at training camp, I was assigned to a minor rank in the Golani Brigade, one of the most highly decorated infantry units in the IDF, responsible for military security in the north. I served in that unit for three years, slowly gaining skills and experience.

At the end of my third year, I had another big decision to make. I could leave the army, having served my time, and go back to civilian life, or re-enlist with the IDF. After weighing all pros and cons, it wasn't that tough a call. I had made progress over my three years in the army. I had a profession and clear goals. So I signed the papers and made the commitment to be a career officer, a decision I've never regretted. Military service is tough and sometimes very dangerous. But it is also extremely rewarding. You always feel you are doing important work, engaged on a great mission to protect your family, your friends, and your nation. With no disrespect intended to troops in other countries, the reality is, being a soldier in Israel means you will almost certainly see action. The Middle East is, plain and simple, one of the most dangerous neighbourhoods in the world. And with Israel being such a small country, we had to be on constant alert. Unlike in huge countries such as Canada or the United States, an invasion of Israel could mean losing the entire country in a matter of days. So even during "peace times," the war never actually stopped for us. There was always shelling and shooting of some kind. If it had happened in another country, you'd call it a war. We called it normal. We certainly never felt safe, even inside our military camps. A grenade could come flying out of nowhere at any time. Letting your guard down even for a second could cost lives and often did.

For example, suppose I was home with my family some weekend, but wanted to visit friends or other relatives. I first had to inform my commanding officers as to where I was going, how long I intended to stay there, and how they could reach me in case of emergency. They needed to know my whereabouts every minute of the day. You were never really off duty.

Speaking of family, we were adding to ours. Shuli got married to a woman he met in Italy named Pnina. She eventually made it to Israel and joined him while he was still in the army. Shuli did two years of military service, then started working at a factory, while at the same time, tried to find a way to build a career as a singer. Dudi had also moved his family to Israel in 1950, so the three brothers were reunited again. But times were tough when Dudi arrived. The economy was going through a recession and he had a tough time finding a decent job. He ended up doing manual labour for various construction companies. Dudi never feared doing hard work, but given the economy, he just couldn't make enough money to make ends meet. I helped him a little from my military salary, but, of course, that didn't deal with the main issue — his frustration at being unable to provide for his family, and finding something he really wanted to do. What he really wanted to do was sing, but as you might imagine, back then, there was never a shortage of cantors at Israeli synagogues.

Shuli and Dudi both had beautiful voices, although very different styles. Shuli had taken some formal training in Italy, which really improved his voice. So not only did he have the natural gifts of a great singer, but he could also add performance skills and artistry to his repertoire. Shuli was always in demand and welcomed in synagogues across the country.

Dudi's voice was different. It wasn't as professional sounding as Shuli's, but when he sang, people literally cried. He had a real depth and sincerity in his singing that touched people's hearts. But, unfortunately, he never had a chance to show his talent to a wider audience in Israel. Eventually, after years of struggling, Dudi and Olga made the hard decision to try their luck somewhere else. Even though it was their decision, it would turn out to have a profound impact on my life as well.

Their new country of choice was Canada.

In 1957, Dudi and his family moved to Montreal, where he quickly established himself as one of the best cantors in that city. It was a good decision to pick Canada for that and so many other reasons as well.

Now, dear reader, let me ask you a question. How many eighteen-year-olds do you know who've jumped out of a plane with a parachute eighteen times? I'm guessing not many. But I did it. In my case it wasn't mandatory — an artillery unit commander could hardly be expected to be dropped from a plane onto territory behind enemy lines. But it was part of the IDF's strategy, aimed at diversifying and improving our skills. But the real reason I agreed to do it was they paid an extra bonus. The prospect of diving from a plane didn't excite me, to say the least. But I needed the money so I did it. Sometimes, I jumped on my own. Other times, they literally threw me out of the plane! Anyway, the whistle of the wind in my ears and queasiness in my stomach weren't pleasant. However, once I felt the pull of the rope, then a sharp jolt, and the parachute canopy opening above me, it was all good. I always landed safely on my feet and, fortunately, the worst injury I ever sustained jumping was once biting my tongue when I hit the ground.

Hundreds of soldiers went through my unit. I greeted them upon their arrival to our territory, trained them, sometimes led them into a fight, and then wished them good luck and said goodbye when their service term ended. Serving in the artillery wasn't in and of itself particularly dangerous. We did have technical superiority over our Arab enemies. We could position our guns at a distance that we knew our opponents' fire couldn't reach, while we bombarded their locations. Of course, there were still many other dangers, from fighter planes attacking us from the air to troops on the ground that could advance unexpectedly and assault our positions. But our air defense and ground forces did a great job protecting us from those threats.

The real danger came during reconnaissance operations, when we had to find an effective and safe position for our guns. There was always the chance of running into a group of soldiers from the other side, or stepping into a minefield. The safety of my people was always my highest priority, so I took all precautions available to avoid unnecessary risk. However, with minefields there was often no choice. Sometimes to accomplish a military mission, I had to risk lives. At that time, there was only one option for a unit facing the task of crossing a minefield — call for volunteers who will go ahead and find a safe way between the mines. It was a horrible thing to ask my men to put their lives on the line in this way, but amazingly, I never had a shortage of volunteers. Back then, and even today as I think about it, I can feel a lump in my throat at the image of a soldier volunteering to step forward towards his possible death. I will never forget those brave people.

Perhaps the most courageous of all the men I ever had under my command was someone named Izhak. We were around the same age, and he was not just another soldier; he was a dear friend as well. Izhak came to Israel from Yugoslavia, thereby managing to avoid the Nazi camps and ghettos. It seemed nothing could scare him. He exuded courage. Sometimes I had to tell him to slow down and take a step back: "Izhak, it's not your turn. Relax, there will be another day and another mission when we will need you."

And there always was. Once, while making our way across a minefield, his partner (another soldier from my unit) stepped on a mine and it exploded, killing him instantly. Izhak was walking first and had somehow avoided the mine by a few inches.

Izhak would set out to do any task fearlessly, whether for a real military operation or just a training mission. When it came to parachute jumping, he chose a free jump, meaning he had to pull his ripcord himself. That's a lot of pressure on a rookie — knowing when to pull the cord himself rather than a controlled jump when the cord is pulled automatically. That was Izhak. Unfortunately, I lost track of him after he left the army and returned to civilian life. What a guy.

I'm so grateful that he survived all the predicaments I put him in, because there is nothing worse for a commander than telling a soldier's parents that their son has died on your watch. I had to perform that duty a few times. It was awful.

You never want to lose a man in battle, but it was even worse to have someone die by accident on your watch. Once there was a fire in my unit's camp. A young soldier was cleaning the tents and accidentally caused a gas explosion. The place was instantly engulfed in flames. I rushed into the fire without hesitation, hoping to save lives. In hindsight, it was probably a more dangerous situation than most of the battles I fought. Luckily, the only damage I suffered was a couple of small burns and the taste of smoke and ashes in my throat and lungs that made me cough for a few days. I could have suffocated, or been hit by a falling beam, or engulfed by the fire — that's exactly how people die in those circumstances. But I was young and brave — or young and stupid, who knows which. I pulled several people out of the burning tents. Some were already just half-conscious from smoke, burns, and shock. Soon the blaze was put out, but we lost three young soldiers in that fire. I accompanied the bodies to their parents' care. Looking into the eyes of a mother or father and telling them what had happened was one of the worst experiences in my entire life, and by far the worst of my military career.

Of course, there were losses in wars as well. We always assumed some of us would not be returning when we engaged the enemy. I remember one confrontation when fifteen commanders — the best officers of our brigade — were killed fighting against the Egyptians. Fifteen good, experienced men. It would take years of training and combat to replace that military wisdom. Losses among the rank and file were much higher. I still blame myself for every lost soldier. Could I have done something differently and saved their lives? I don't think so, but one never knows. Sometimes, war is war, and it's your job to protect your country at all costs. I always hoped I led by example — being that first guy to step out of the trench, the first to hear the bullets whistling past your ears. I think my men trusted me to do that, and as a result, they followed me out of the hole.

Most of the time, military discipline had to be strict, particularly with young soldiers. I insisted they stay with the unit 24/7, no exceptions. I needed them to be ready and available in case of an attack. I also wanted them safe and thought their chances of staying alive were better when they were with me. But one night, a soldier came to me, looking absolutely desperate. He said he absolutely needed a pass to go outside and visit his hometown. He had left a girl at home and now, after not having seen him for such a long time, she wrote him a letter threatening that if he didn't get his tail back home to see her the next weekend, she would break up with him. This guy was madly in love with the girl. But that wasn't the issue. The issue was, what the heck was I supposed to do? According to the rules, it was an open and shut case: forget it, you're staying here. But this was about a girl!

I told him to report to me the next Sunday night and wished him good luck.

Was I was risking a lot? Absolutely. What if my superior officer dropped by to take attendance, or the kid did something stupid while on leave, or didn't come back on time, or at all? It seemed like a lot more bad things could have happened than good ones. But you have to trust people if you want them to trust you. It's not an exaggeration to say that without this trust between soldiers and commanders, wars cannot be won. Strong armies begin with the small things that lead to big victories.

If you asked me to pick the most significant of the campaigns I took part in, I'd choose the Suez Crisis. For those of you too young to remember, the Suez Crisis took place over a week in late October to early November in 1956. Historians say it marked the end of Great Britain's being considered one of the world's great powers. It was the culmination of a series of tit-for-tat moves involving the United States, the Soviet Union, Britain, France, Egypt, and Israel, and of course, it was all about oil.

In a nutshell, here's what happened. When Gamal Abdel Nasser became the second president of Egypt in June 1956, he reoriented the country's interests more towards the Soviet Union. As a result, several Western countries, which had financially backed the building of the Aswan Dam, withdrew their funding. Nasser retaliated by nationalizing the Suez Canal. Western powers saw that move as an attempt to choke off their access to Middle Eastern oil, and so they conspired to regain Western control of the canal and remove Nasser from power. Israel invaded Egypt, then Britain and France began to bomb Cairo. Leaders in all three countries insisted their actions were in response to Nasser's moves, but there was evidence that the invasion was planned well before any of these moves had happened. Britain and France had egg on their faces, the Americans and Soviets pressured them to cease military activities, which they did, but not before the Soviets threatened the United Kingdom and France with nuclear strikes. British Prime Minister Anthony Eden was accused of misleading Parliament and subsequently resigned. Nasser remained in power until his death in 1970.

My unit was stationed in Al Arish on the Sinai Peninsula and we faced the harshest and toughest combat I'd ever experienced. It was there that we suffered that fluke explosion that claimed the lives of three of our soldiers, the ones who burned to death. Our Golani Brigade suffered other serious losses — many people were killed or wounded. But I remember the Suez Crisis for more than just military reasons. During that war, I met the woman who would become my wife.

Here's how it happened. During a brief ceasefire, our senior commanders thought they'd give us a break from the war so they organized a visit to our unit by a group of young teachers. I think the idea was to let us interact with some pretty girls and allow us to forget about the hardships of the war for a while. I was, to say the least, rather inexperienced when it came to women, but I did something to make myself irresistible: I attached two massive handguns to my belt!

It actually worked perfectly. Everyone wanted to dance with me, everyone flirted with me and laughed at my jokes even before I opened my mouth. Was I a little bit drunk as well? Who knows, maybe yes! It was after the war, we were all in Israel, and everyone was happy. So yes, I was a bit of a hit with the women — at least, almost all the women. There was this one girl, maybe a bit shy, maybe a little intimidated by the large company. She had practically chained herself to the wall and was too embarrassed to mingle with the rest of the dancing crowd. If she wanted to attract my attention she picked the best approach. I thought she definitely deserved a closer look. I walked over to her and asked her for a dance. I know this is completely crazy to say, but I tell you it's true: by the end of that party, I knew that she would be my wife.

I asked her name and where she lived. She reluctantly told me that she lived somewhere around Kiryat Borochov in the vicinity of Ramat Gan, but I'm not sure that I managed to get her last name out of her.

Once the party was over, the girls went back home, and we returned to our positions on the front line until the war finally ended. A month or two later I got some vacation time and decided to find that girl. Ilana was her name. But before I could pursue her, I had to take stock of where I was in my life. I had to admit to myself that, despite having achieved a certain level of success — I was an officer in charge of a large anti-tank unit with the trust of my subordinates and higher commanders — I still couldn't see a path to climbing higher up the career ladder.

One of my problems was a lack of education. I was taken out of school by the Nazis at eleven, and had only studied a little in Italy. After that, I was too busy making a living and had no spare time for textbooks. Without at least a high school diploma, it was pointless to hope for further promotions.

There was also the *Altalena* stigma that had haunted me from my first day in Israel. Ironically, one of my fondest memories, something I was so deeply proud of, put me at a disadvantage every time it came to choosing between me and other officers for career advancement. Most of the higher officers were members of the Haganah, the main paramilitary group in Mandatory Palestine. In their eyes, I simply wasn't a reliable person.

I knew I wanted to have a family, just like the sweet, loving family I once had in Dej. I wanted a wife and kids. The moment I saw Ilana, I knew she was the one for me, and I somehow sensed that she wanted the same things that I did.

I can't remember whether I found Ilana on the first day of my search or the next one, but I did find her. I arrived at the right address and knocked on the right door. She opened the door and literally froze in the doorway. I guess she wasn't expecting me.

She couldn't turn me away, so in I came for a chat. I decided that the best strategy was to be open and honest. I told her I was a serious guy, that I wanted to have a family, and that all my intentions were honest. Her mother was somewhat helpful to my ambitions. I learned after the fact that my future mother-in-law told her daughter that it was obvious I was serious about marriage, and that if Ilana wasn't, she should let me know so I didn't waste my time. In any event, I guess I was persuasive enough, and we soon started dating.

Ilana was born Liliana Perlberg in Poland (she changed her first name to Ilana after moving to Israel). When the Germans invaded Poland on September 1, 1939, to launch the Second World War, she was only two years old. Her mother, Sara, was a smart and strong woman, whose intelligence combined with an exceptional intuition. Sara knew terrible times lay ahead, and therefore decided on a risky plan in hopes of protecting her family. She saw two evils — Nazi Germany to the west, and the Soviet Union to the east — but she thought her chances for survival were better in the communist country. So she started looking for a way to cross the border with her husband Leon, who was smart enough to listen.

They took Ilana and left Lodz, where the family lived, and made for a small town near the Soviet-Polish border where one of Sara's relatives, a dentist, lived. That dentist provided the family with temporary shelter as they prepared for the next leg of their journey. They found a guide, paid him to take them to the right place, bribed guards at the border control, and were let out of Poland. Yes, what they did was illegal and so technically, they could be prosecuted for their transgression. But at the time there were hundreds of Jews running from Poland to the Soviet Union, and the authorities turned a blind eye in dealing with many of them.

Eventually, the family settled in Uzbekistan, one of the republics inside the Soviet Union (now an independent country), and they lived in many different cities, including the capital, Tashkent. Leon, who had stayed behind, was soon recruited into the Polish Army formed by the Soviets to fight the Nazis on the East. He went through the entire war, and ultimately liberated his home country, Poland.

Sara and Ilana, meanwhile, went through many hardships in Uzbekistan. There were no jobs and they suffered from terrible living conditions and hunger — sometimes they had nothing to eat at all. But somehow, Sara managed to get her daughter through that awful time. The only resources they could rely on were the things they had brought with them from Poland: Sara's dresses, kitchen silver, and some jewelry. Sara would go to the market and exchange an item or two for bread, potatoes, or rice. This is how they survived until the end of the war, after which they went back to Lodz and reunited with Leon.

Of course, there wasn't much of a Jewish community to return to in Lodz. Only a tiny fraction of the more than two hundred thousand Jews returned. The rest were murdered in the ghettos and camps.

Soon after the war, Ilana's parents started thinking about moving to Israel, and in 1948, when the Jewish state declared its independence, they decided to leave Poland. (In addition, Ilana had two brothers: Alex, who died at birth, and Roni who was fourteen years her junior.) It was a difficult decision because the Polish government insisted immigrants had to leave practically everything behind. Though they were allowed to sell their little apartment, they were forced to accept a ridiculously low price for it. Ilana wanted to take her favourite bike with her to Israel, but even that wasn't permitted. However, little Ilana didn't want to take no for an answer. She wrote a letter to the country's prime minister explaining to him that this bike was a birthday present from her parents and she didn't want to leave it behind. It was a precious souvenir and reminder of her home country and childhood that she desperately wanted to keep. She placed a stamp on the envelope and dropped it in the mailbox. Her parents had a really hard time explaining to her why she shouldn't expect an answer, and of course, she didn't get one. The family set off with very little luggage, but the police at the border control ransacked even that. Anything of value was confiscated.

In Israel, things got better. They were lucky to avoid being sent to one of the "tent camps" for newcomers, as was the normal practice practise due to a housing shortage. New settlers would sometimes live for months in a "tent town" before moving to an apartment. When the weather was very hot, that wasn't a pleasant experience at all. But there was simply no way to accommodate everyone quickly. Hundreds of people arrived in Israel every day, and so these temporary dwellings were the only solution. Ilana's family was luckier than most, and right after their arrival they moved to Ramat Gan on the eastern outskirts of Tel Aviv, where Sara's brother Nathan lived. At first, they stayed with him, but since he worked as a supervisor at an apartment house and knew the drill, Nathan helped them get a small apartment in the town. Ilana's parents found jobs and established a normal life. Ilana herself went to school and after finishing chose to become a teacher.

Ilana and I dated for about a year and a half, and then, on March 17, 1958, we got married at an army club at a military encampment somewhere between Jaffa and Tel Aviv. For this occasion, I decided to get out of my uniform. An army chaplain performed the ceremony. And of course, there was a crowd of my colleagues and friends in uniforms. We had invited lots of guests, two hundred or so, I think. Ilana's friends and parents came. Dudi couldn't be present, because by that time he had already left Israel and was living in Montreal. But my other brother Shuli, his wife Pnina, and their new daughter Elka were there. (Elka, of course, was named after my mother.) There was also one man from Dej. I had met him in Israel and even though he wasn't a close friend, I invited him because I wanted someone else from my hometown to be at my wedding.

As wonderful as the wedding was, we almost didn't have one. Money was the issue. My in-laws tried to talk us out of having one because they didn't have much money, and paying for the event would have been a huge burden. Nevertheless, we went through with the wedding, paid for it with our own money, but still got a fabulous wedding gift from my in-laws — a refrigerator. Back then in Israel, it was a truly exceptional, luxurious gift. Having a refrigerator in your apartment was as rare as owning a car. So my in-laws were really fantastic.

I got a loan from the army to pay for the wedding — there was a special fund for soldiers, and I could pay off the debt over time on a monthly basis. I also had a bit of savings. As an army officer, I had a good salary compared to what the average Israeli earned, and as a member of the Golani Brigade, I was paid a little better than our colleagues in other branches of the army.

Buying into the Zionist dream back then was not like today. Today, Israel is known as the "Start-Up Nation" for its tremendous success in high technology businesses. Back then, salaries were much smaller compared to those in developed countries. Only a tiny minority, maybe 5 percent at most, could afford an apartment, and yet somehow I found myself in that elite group. I never turned down a chance to make extra money, whether it was throwing myself out of airplanes with a parachute on my back, or learning another language. That's right: the government gave us a little bonus to learn another language, so I studied Arabic. There were also some money-saving perks for the military. For example, we received a 50 percent discount on all shows, including movies. With the money I had stashed away from my salary, I bought an apartment on Radak Street in Ramat Gan. It was a small place, just a room and a half really. I got a folding bed and that was all my furniture. Owning an apartment was a very important argument in convincing Ilana's parents to approve our marriage. When they asked where we were going to live if we got married, I was able to tell them proudly that I had a place of my own. It was a big deal back then.

So after the wedding, when all the guests had finally left, Ilana and I went to our little nest on Radak Street. I remember that I couldn't eat at the wedding because I was too excited and too nervous, so when we came home, I was starving. The only food I could find in my bachelor apartment was schmaltz herring. I devoured it and enjoyed every piece.

No, we didn't get to go on a honeymoon because I was busy with my army duties. There was no chance of getting a month-long vacation. Later though, we spent a week together at a nice resort in Nahariya, Israel's northernmost coastal city.

Ilana taught school in Ramat Gan. I continued my military service, teaching young soldiers how to operate anti-tank guns. We started with twenty-five millimetre Hotchkiss guns, French-made weapons that were widely used during the Second World War, and then eventually, as the army grew more experienced and professional, and as military technologies developed, changed to more sophisticated and efficient weaponry.

Whenever I had the chance, I visited my brother Shuli. He was living in Ramat HaSharon, another small city near Tel Aviv, about fifteen kilometres from our home. He was working as a cantor in one of the local synagogues and also did some work as a political activist, promoting the ideals and vision of Menachem Begin and his Herut party, the precursor to the Likud coalition. I went to some of the meetings he organized, and at one of them, met Begin again. It was a small gathering of maybe twenty or thirty people during an election campaign. Begin made one of his passionate speeches for which he was so famous. My commander thought attending that campaign event was a big mistake. Of course, almost all of the senior military leaders were adherents of David Ben Gurion's Mapai party, and they clearly frowned upon anyone who supported anything else. My attitude was, it was my private time and I would use it in any way I wanted.

Whenever I felt Menachem Begin needed support, I tried to go to public events and rallies that he held. In 1952, there was a serious controversy in Israel over the financial compensation Germany had offered to pay for the genocide committed by the Nazis. It was a hard time in Israel, the country was in an economic crisis, the unemployment rate was high, and the government desperately needed money to speed up the recovery. Ben Gurion wanted to take money from the Germans. Begin disagreed. He believed when it came to the Holocaust, any bargaining was unacceptable. When he announced that a rally would be held against the deal with the German government, I knew I had to be there. Once again, I took off my uniform and put on my civilian clothes. A huge crowd gathered in Tel Aviv —about fifteen thousand people. Begin delivered one of his most emotional and moving speeches ever. He stood on a stand with a sign that read: "Our honour shall not be sold for money. Our blood shall not be atoned by goods. We shall wipe out the disgrace." On the *Altalena*, he had called on his supporters not to return fire — the unity of the nation was more important. But now he called on his followers to voice their disagreement with the government that was going to take blood money. The crowd responded by chanting his name and protesting against the government's plans.

I marched with the others. I had to be careful not to get in trouble. If arrested, it would automatically mean the end of my military career. But I knew I had come to that rally because I strongly believed that Begin was right. We shouldn't have taken the money because there simply was not enough money in the world to compensate us for what the Nazis did. You couldn't measure that suffering in dollars, marks, or shekels. Accepting the compensation, in my view, was akin to admitting that what had happened was after all "only about money." But Ben Gurion got his way, and Germany did compensate Israel. In fact, many of the public transit buses and taxi cabs in Israel are made by Mercedes-Benz, one of Germany's most successful car companies, and one which prospered during the Second World War thanks to its strong support of Nazism. The company also used thousands of slaves, many of whom were Jews.

I didn't take my share of the money from the German government until many years later, only after I had retired and moved to Canada. You see, in the early years after the war, we had feared that the Holocaust's place in history and the culpability of the perpetrators would be papered over by payouts from the Germans. But over the years, the Jewish world had done a great deal to ensure that would not be the case. So it seemed more reasonable to accept compensation to rebuild the Jewish lives of those whose existence had been shattered during the war.

Incidentally, that Herut demonstration did get out of hand and the police eventually used tear gas to disperse the crowd. The rally ended with clashes between police and protesters. Luckily, I avoided any trouble and returned to my unit safely.

Army, politics, and family were the chief concerns shaping my life. We were paying down our debts, buying some furniture, and waiting for the addition of a new member to our family. Less than a year after we got married, on December 6, 1958, my son Moshe was born in Petah Tikva, a small sleepy town a few kilometres east of Tel Aviv. He was named after my father. Ilana and I had a little debate over the name. She wanted something more modern, but eventually with her parents' persuasion, she came to agree with me.

As the 1950s were wrapping up, I was a regiment sergeant instructor at an officers' school. I was in charge of about five hundred people in my unit — many more than an officer of my level would be normally put in charge of. So I was actually doing a higher-ranked officer's job, and under different circumstances, should have been promoted to the next officer rank.

But that never happened for me and you know why. Nevertheless, looking back at my military career, I don't think I would have changed a thing. I was a soldier when Israel needed soldiers the most. I'm proud of the job I've done as an officer in the Israeli army. It is a very special army in so many ways — clearly, it's one of the best in the world. I know this first-hand because I participated in building it from scratch, from unprofessional and naive into an efficient, dangerous, well-educated and well-trained force. It's now armed with state-of-the-art equipment and technologies, and with its experienced and skilled soldiers, the Israeli army continues to secure the safety of the nation.

Every rookie is taught from the first day in the army the main principle: you cannot shoot a non-combatant. Your target can only be a member of the opposing army, someone with a gun or any other weapon pointed at you, someone you have no other choice but to kill, otherwise he would kill you. "Watch before you shoot," and "think twice before you shoot" are the watchwords of the IDF. I truly believe this is a force motivated not by hatred, but by the sense of responsibility for the nation, for families, relatives, and friends. It's been formed to protect people. The troops know what they are fighting for — their only home, their only nation.

# 8

# Maple Syrup

By 1966 I had served eighteen years in the Israel Defense Forces, and I was coming to the realization that I was running out of time. I was approaching my mid-thirties and found I really couldn't enjoy my growing family as much as I wanted to because of my military duties. Yes, my family was growing. On March 9, 1964, our second son Dan was born. Ilana wasn't happy with my being away from home so much. Often, I was only around once or twice a month.

There was another factor that was gnawing at me as well. When I was a single, young kid, I wasn't afraid of anything. I embraced the dangerous situations I found myself in while doing my military duties. But those single days were gone. I now had the three dearest people in the world to me constantly waiting for me to return from a military operation or a training camp. I certainly tried to reduce the number of risky situations I put myself in, but the fact was, every time a soldier leaves home, he understands it could be for the last time. Who would take care of my family then? I had already more than contributed to my country's military needs and was proud of my service. It was time to think about the next chapter of my life.

So that's what was on my mind when my brother Dudi, whom I hadn't seen in years, sent me some airplane tickets and an invitation to visit him in Montreal. I had six weeks of vacation time banked so the timing was perfect.

"Motke," he added, "think about moving to Canada. I'll help you."

Move to Canada? I couldn't imagine it. At the time of the invitation, I wasn't yet sure I was ready to leave the army. Nor could I believe that Ilana would leave her parents and relatives behind. Moreover, Shuli and his family were still in Israel and he had no plans to leave. Visit Canada? By all means. Move there? Not a chance.

It was a wonderful time to visit the world's second largest country, and what a contrast with Israel, one of the world's smallest and most vulnerable nations. Canada was a year away from celebrating its Centennial, and there seemed to be a great spirit and pride in the land. Some things were obvious from the moment we arrived in Montreal. The people were nice. The standard of living was higher than in Israel. The sense of security, even with increasing tensions from Quebec separatists, was in stark contrast to life in Israel, where we expected war to break out at any moment. Of course, we became accustomed to living with that threat over our heads all the time in Israel, but still, the peacefulness of Canada

— having that longest undefended border in the world with the United States — was refreshing.

Strangely enough, I didn't go for two of Canada's best-known international delicacies: maple syrup and ice wine. They were both too sweet and sugary for me. Like most eastern Europeans, I like saltier fare. But I have to confess, Canada made a great impression on me.

We returned to Israel after a very satisfying trip and with one more year remaining on my contract with the army. But my mind kept returning to Canada. The happy memories of that trip just never left me. With three months left in my army contract, I was scheduled to be interviewed to figure out what would come next. Naturally, the army brass figured I would want to extend my contract again, although someone did advise me that if I really wanted to leave, now was a good time. So Ilana and I had a lengthy discussion about it. This was one of those moments in life where you get to a fork in the road. Do we stay and embark on a third decade of living in Israel? Or do we try something very different in the "new world"?

It was 1967, just before yet another military confrontation with our Arab neighbours that would come to be known as the Six Day War. Although that war would represent the greatest military triumph in Israel's history, the country's economy was in a deep recession, and leaving the military for what seemed like precious few employment opportunities in the civilian world didn't make much sense.

Then we got a final piece of advice that helped us make our decision. Our oldest son Moshe was suffering from asthma. His doctors told us he could really benefit from moving to a different climate. Dudi was still encouraging us from Montreal to make the move. And so, we did. I retired from the army, and walked out of my unit's barracks into civilian life. What an odd feeling after more than twenty years serving in the military. Two months after leaving the military, I received my army pension and with that, we were off to Montreal.

The plan was to come to Canada on a trial basis. We would stay for a couple of years and then re-evaluate our decision. Frankly, we couldn't imagine living outside Israel for long and guessed that in two years, we'd be moving back.

The world was about to descend upon Montreal to help Canada celebrate its one hundredth birthday when we arrived in Montreal. It was called Expo '67 and it turned out to be perhaps the most successful world's fair ever. So many countries built impressive-looking pavilions in Montreal, and it seemed as if much of Canada came for a visit. Space exploration was a particularly hot topic at the time, so thousands of people came to see the Apollo and Vostok exhibits. Buckminster Fuller designed an unforgettable geodesic dome for the American pavilion, Canada had its innovative Katimavik pavilion, and the province of Ontario had one as well. It was a fantastic display of cutting edge design and it was all happening in Montreal.

While the world focused on Expo, Dudi and I set our gaze on a much more mundane idea to make some money. My brother was making a living as a cantor at one of Montreal's synagogues, but he was also looking for an opportunity to supplement that income. Expo '67 provided that opportunity.

What was I going to bring to this venture? Actually, not too much if you're talking about experience in the business world.

I was a soldier, not a businessman. My one bit of experience in that world involved selling key chains bearing the images of Israeli political leaders and models of Israel's new parliament building during the brief period between leaving the army and moving to Montreal. For a short time, I had a job as a vendor, selling souvenir models of the building. I didn't have a car, but I found a guy who did. I couldn't drive, but he couldn't sell, so we teamed up and shared the profits. I didn't make a fortune, but collected some decent pocket money. But that was a far cry from the business venture Dudi now wanted me to embrace.

My brother rented several parking lots in Montreal. With massive numbers of tourists arriving daily, he thought we could make some serious cash. He wanted me to run one of his lots. Not too complicated, you might say. Well, true, except that I didn't speak any French, and my English was lousy, despite taking lessons in the evening. But I figured it out and we did make some decent money while Expo was on.

After staying with Dudi's family for a few weeks, Ilana and I then rented our own apartment on Boulevard Décarie (it had a pretty decent population of young Jewish families at the time) and I started to consider what else I could do in Canada. We wanted to give Canada a real shot, but we also knew that if it didn't work out, Israel was always waiting for us to return. In fact, we stashed some money away and promised ourselves never to touch it — that was our return plane fare to Israel just in case. We also had kept our apartment in Ramat Gan near Tel Aviv, despite having received numerous good offers to sell it. Instead, we rented it out, Ilana's parents kept an eye on it for us, and it was always there in case we needed it again.

After the excitement and intensity of Expo was behind us, we decided that we really needed to get to know this new country of ours better. The contrasts with Israel continued to amaze us. We couldn't get over how gorgeous the forests, mountains, and rivers were. The landscapes seemed to go on forever. Remember, there are some parts of Israel where you can drive across the width of the entire country in half an hour. We couldn't even drive across Montreal in half an hour.

One of our new friends —another immigrant from Israel named Zusia — suggested we take a snowmobile trip. My boys loved the idea. So on a gorgeous, sunny winter morning, we rented two snowmobiles and set off for something completely new for us — a picnic on snow banks.

Our expedition went extremely well, until the inevitable happened — we got lost. The kids thought it was a terribly exciting adventure, especially when we had to hide out in an abandoned farmhouse to shelter ourselves from the rising winds and ensuing blizzard. We couldn't find any matches to light a fire and suddenly, excitement gave way to concern. The kids were getting hungry and cold and their feet were freezing. If this were happening today, you'd say we all felt like contestants on an episode of that reality TV program *Survivor*. At this point, my army experience kicked in. I told the kids, who were quite skeptical of this advice, to take off their shoes and start vigorously rubbing their feet. Next, I managed to start a fire the old fashioned way — rubbing two sticks together. It took a long time and cost me some blisters on the palms of my hands, but I got it done. We hunkered down around the fire, figuring we'd be waiting hours and hours for help. Fortunately, my friend

Zusia's wife, Tziona, was concerned that we didn't return at the appointed hour, so she sent out a rescue team, which soon got on our trail, and eventually (and mercifully) found us.

Montreal, at this time, was a big rich city with lots of opportunity. Today, it's definitely a distant second place to Toronto as Canada's premier city. But back then, we were still nearly a decade away from René Lévesque's separatist party winning government, prompting an exodus of people and businesses that were afraid of what that government might do.

Having said all that, we were still genuinely undecided about whether to stay. Ironically, Dudi and his family were now thinking of moving to the United States. Despite the success he was enjoying in Montreal, he had been sending audiotapes of his singing to synagogues across the border. Dudi was ambitious; he wanted more, and I didn't blame him. Even with his decent job in Montreal, I thought he was earning well below his market value and abilities. He deserved to work for a larger, more prestigious congregation in the U.S.

But where did that leave us? We did like Montreal, but one thing constantly gnawed at me. I started to feel as if I were even more of a stranger than I truly was because I didn't speak French very well. I certainly had no problem trying to learn the language. After all, I already spoke Yiddish, Hungarian, Italian, Hebrew, German, a bit of Polish and Arabic, and now some English. But I didn't like the feeling of being almost a second-class citizen. I had no problem with Quebec trying to maintain its distinctiveness by insisting on policies that favored the French language. I had a bit of a problem with what I saw as increasingly anti-English policies, particularly since Quebec is a province in Canada and English is one of the country's official languages. It started to feel to me that Quebec nationalism was increasingly trying to divide people according to race or language, and I thought the consequences of that could be damaging to the country. I came to the conclusion that I didn't feel comfortable living in this kind of environment, and as I suggested earlier, I wasn't the only one. Once the Parti Québécois won power in 1976, it was a common sight to see moving vans heading west down Canada's busiest highway, the 401, as Quebec lost thousands of its citizens. We didn't wait that long. Toronto was really the first and only place we considered moving to, because Ilana had a cousin who already lived there. His name was Arthur Logan and he owned a small jewelry business. Also, the fact that Toronto's climate was a little less unforgiving than Montreal's didn't hurt. I'll never forget arriving in Montreal for the first time to snow that was up to our knees. For us Israelis, that was a pretty intense experience.

While all of Canada welcomed a new prime minister in 1968 (Pierre Elliott Trudeau), Toronto welcomed our little family to its midst. We rented an apartment near Beth Sholom Synagogue on Eglinton Avenue (it's at the foot of the Allen Expressway, which had not yet been built when we moved there). For all of you renters, imagine this: we moved into a new building and therefore, the owners needed to give people an incentive to move in. So they gave us the first three or four months rent-free. That was typical back then. Today, they want the first and last month's rent paid in advance.

One of the habits we'd picked up since the end of the Second World War was never to completely unpack our things, regardless of where we lived. I guess the experience of having troops knock on our family's door in Dej, then giving us half an hour to pack our belongings and get out, had a lasting impact on me. As a result, we hadn't unpacked most of our stuff after arriving in Montreal — just the bare necessities. We didn't actually think Nazi troops would knock on our door in Montreal, but you can understand where this anxiety comes from. Once we got to Toronto, there was something about the place that just made us feel very welcomed. So what did we do? We finally unpacked everything. It was a positive sign.

Our cousin Arthur was very helpful, giving me a chance to test my business abilities in his jewelry business. Since I already knew the city of Montreal relatively well, he suggested I start there, going from store to store, offering our merchandise for sale. Arthur was buying jewelry in Europe and then trading it through agents across Canada. From every sale I would get a commission — 10 percent. Arthur gave me five suitcases of his wares and off on a road trip I went. It may sound like I was carrying a small fortune with me but in fact, the diamonds weren't real: it was costume jewelry. So I didn't have reason to be afraid of thieves.

In Montreal, I wasted no time going from store to store, following the list I got from Arthur. I did seem to have a bit of a knack in making sales, and things went really well. I called back to Toronto to report to Arthur as to how I was doing, and when he heard the numbers, he thought I was kidding. I sold about two thousand dollars' worth of goods in two days. It may not sound like much today, but back then, the commission on that was enough to pay my rent for a month.

Nevertheless, I kept looking for other opportunities. I'd check the classified ads in the newspapers, call hundreds of businesses, and get called into dozens of interviews every month. I may have embellished my qualifications a tad (fluent in French? Of course!), but I really wanted to start doing something I loved and providing better for my family.

Real estate started to intrigue me, so I took a course and got some training in the trade. Today, of course, prices in Toronto are sky-high and there are often crazy bidding wars on houses. Not so four decades ago, when the market was much quieter and a 3 percent commission didn't amount to much. But I was determined to make a go of it, so I worked hard knocking on doors, negotiating deals, and scouring Toronto neighbourhoods for potential business. But after doing this for several months, I came to realize this wouldn't be enough to provide well for Ilana and the kids.

Even as I tried other options, I never stopped working for Arthur. I needed that income to stay afloat, and, bit by bit, learned a lot of the tricks on how to run a business: attention to detail, diligence in collecting, dreaming up new and creative ways to sell our merchandise. I always listened carefully to store owners for exactly what they wanted on the assumption that they knew their customers as well, if not better than I did.

In the 1970s there were lots of Jewish-owned variety stores in downtown Toronto and the owners all loved doing two things: selling jewelry to their customers, and talking shop with me. And I was a good listener. I learned more about the business world, then started going to international fairs where I learned about new trends in the market, new fashions, and new technologies.

Gradually, I became more and more experienced in the field and thought, why shouldn't I open my own business? I could just as easily bring in products from Europe, and then sell them in Canada. When I told Arthur this, he was a total gentleman. Many others would have been miffed at having to deal with a new competitor. Instead, he gave me his blessing. In Yiddish, we call this kind of guy a mensch — a person of integrity and honour.

I opened my own company — Ronen Distribution. It really was a family affair. Ilana helped manage the office and covered for me whenever I was away on a road trip; and it worked really well. At first, Ilana and I operated out of a room in our home basement. But as each year passed and we continued to do better, we finally bought an office at the corner of Steeles and Keele Avenues in 1980. We were fairly close to a sizeable Italian community at that location, and many Italian-Canadians came to me for wedding gifts such as silver plate giftware and crystal ware. Italian weddings are traditionally huge events with hundreds of guests and many presents. Silver, cut glass, jewelry, and other *bomboniere* were very popular gifts. And when I did business with my Italian customers, I spoke Italian again; I hadn't forgotten the language. Just like the people, the Italian language is beautiful too. Working with Italians always brought back memories of the old days back in postwar Italy, and my first taste of freedom. It was a good time, filled with hopes and good friends.

If I'm making this all sound rather smooth and easy, let me assure you it wasn't. Like all new immigrants, it took a helluva lot of effort, day after day, putting in long hours for a good five years until Ilana and I felt our future was truly safe in Toronto.

And that's just the economic side of the ledger. There was also restarting our lives once again, trying to master a new language, making new friends, learning about Canadian culture and traditions. It was tough. But the hard work and effort paid off. In 1972, we bought a house near Bathurst Street and Steeles Avenue in Toronto, and we still live in the same house. We paid forty-two thousand dollars for it. Today, that wouldn't even buy you an outhouse in the backyard. Back then, it felt as if we were spending a fortune, but to us, Canada was worth it. We even tapped into that money we swore we wouldn't touch, in case we needed to high tail it back to Israel. Furthermore, despite how tight our financial situation was, we made the decision to put both of our boys into parochial (Jewish day) school. It was very expensive, but gives you some indication of how big a priority we put on a good Jewish education.

Keeping the boys' heritage was important to us. We always spoke Hebrew in the home, so the boys are perfectly bilingual. And we followed our religious traditions, celebrated Shabbat and the holidays.

Ilana and I made up our minds. Toronto was home, and would remain home for many years to come.

If the house was our cake, we celebrated by buying some icing for that cake. For the first time ever, we bought a car. It was a two-door, white 1964 Chevy II. It was a used car; however, the previous owner seemed to have driven hardly more than a couple of victory laps around his house in it — the car had only forty kilometres on the odometer. We paid eight hundred dollars for it, and it was another tangible sign of the progress we had made in Canada. Not even in our most prosperous years in Israel could we have afforded an automobile. Now, we could take family trips visiting our friends inside and outside Toronto.

We travelled to Israel as well. More often than not, Ilana and the boys would go and I'd stay back home to work, or just go for a short time. Life was good. Now, nearly five decades after coming to Canada, our sons have married and have families of their own. And it's so crystal clear that we made the right decision to come to Canada. This may sound odd but we were able to keep the traditions of our Jewish identity despite leaving the Jewish State. In fact, it may have been easier to hang on to our Jewish traditions in Canada than in Israel, where I was away on military duty so often, so was seldom around to observe Shabbat or the holidays. It also seems that in Canada, we made the extra effort to practice our faith because we were so far away from Israel. Israelis don't feel they need to do anything special to be Jewish. They're living in the Holy Land after all. What could be more Jewish than that?

So on Friday nights, Ilana lit Shabbat candles, I said the blessings on the wine and the challah (special Sabbath bread), we regularly went to synagogue, said prayers, and celebrated the holidays. We found it especially beneficial living in a multiethnic, multicultural city such as Toronto. Somehow, it made us that much more aware of our own religion and culture.

We never cut ties with Israel and every time we had the chance, we would visit the country, which we still considered our own, and we celebrated both Moshe and Dan's bar mitzvahs in Israel, that special ceremony that thirteen-year-old Jewish boys experience as they're called to the Torah to "become men."

Canada has become our permanent home and it will be our home for the rest of our lives, however long that may be. I'll admit, it took a bit of time to fall in love with Canada, but now I can't imagine living anywhere else.

I'll make one more confession: as much as I've wanted to, I still can't bring myself to eat maple syrup. It's just too sweet for my eastern-European taste buds!

# 9

## *L'chaim!*

The years passed. My sons grew up. I always wanted them to be hard-working, independent people. And I think our efforts paid off. My sons were surprisingly easy to raise, never giving Ilana or me the difficulties that so many parents have to contend with. I suppose there are several possible explanations for this. Maybe we just got lucky. Maybe our kids were unusually diligent and serious. Maybe they knew of their parents' background and as a result, decided to go easy on us. Who knows? They were certainly normal kids who got into the occasional run-ins with trouble, as all teenagers do. But thankfully, Ilana and I were spared the worst of the typical teenage transgressions.

Dan developed an early interest in sports, particularly basketball and soccer, while Moshe gravitated towards other activities. I think he was only fourteen when he started organizing parties and social events, at home, at school, and even at synagogue. He also started working at an early age. He might have been just fourteen or fifteen when he got himself a job at a gas station. In the winter, he would come home some nights with his hands almost blue from cold, but he was proud that he was making his own money. We tried to teach both boys the importance of saving money, and how it could lead to financial independence.

I look back now at some of the silly things that happened under our roof and I have to laugh. Once, Ilana noticed that something looked wrong with the tiled floor downstairs in our house. It looked warped and the tiles suddenly started to loosen. We were scratching our heads, unable to find an explanation as to what was ruining what seemed like a perfectly solid floor.

Eventually, the boys confessed. It was all Moshe's idea. He had "bribed" Dan to wash the floor, and he did so with water and detergent. Trouble was, the floor wasn't supposed to have contact with liquid at all. Dan, five years younger, was unable to say no to his brother. We had to call in a specialist to fix the floor. The kids repented and were eventually forgiven after promising never to do anything like that again. Besides, it was pretty hard to be angry at a kid who was disappointed with our own standards of hygiene.

Work kept me plenty busy, but I did try to spend more time with my boys. I attended both events organized by Moshe, and the soccer and basketball matches in which Dan played. Dan was so passionate about sports, especially basketball, it led him eventually to transfer schools. Like Moshe, he was going to a Jewish parochial school, but Dan's basketball team wasn't nearly competitive enough for him. He wanted to play in higher-level competitions, and Ilana and I had to respect his ambitions even though it interfered with our plans to give him a thorough Jewish education. We didn't worry about his academic achievements. He always had good marks in all subjects. So we complied with his wishes, sent him to another school, and he successfully played for its tougher team. I did my best not to skip a single game, and he was always very happy to see his father in the bleachers.

Dan and Moshe also got me to try something I had somehow managed to avoid all my life: ice-skating. I guess to be truly Canadian, you've got to learn how to skate, so I gave it a try. Actually, I didn't skate so much as flip and flop all over the ice, but I kept at it and was determined to stay upright until I eventually suffered a serious hand injury. I tried avoiding the doctor's office, but eventually the pain was too intense. I booked an appointment and discovered I'd broken my wrist, which had to be put in a cast. So ended my skating career. But so began my sports-watching career. The kids took me under their wings and I developed an interest in watching hockey games both on television and at the arena.

After graduating from high school, Moshe went to York University in Toronto to study political science and economics. After completing his undergraduate program, he went to the University of Windsor to study law. Windsor was a long way away, and I thought I'd miss him a great deal, but remarkably, he came home almost every week and continued to help me with the business. In his final year, he even transferred back to the Osgoode Hall Law School in Toronto so he could be closer to home. During all his student years, he volunteered with Jewish youth organizations, and was best known for his work with "Network," the informal name of the Jewish Students Network, a large organization coordinating Jewish student activities across the United States and Canada. In 1985, when U.S. President Ronald Reagan went to Bitburg, Germany, and stubbornly insisted on visiting a cemetery where former SS officers were buried, it caused mass protests in Jewish communities around the world. Moshe organized young people in Canada to protest against Reagan's action in the Bitburg cemetery during the President's visit. Moshe actually consulted with Elie Wiesel, the Holocaust survivor and human rights champion, who told Moshe he had a duty to go, to protest the "whitewashing" of who the real victims and real aggressors were in that cemetery. A year later, in 1986, he went to Switzerland with Avital Shcharansky, wife of the world's best known Soviet refusenik Anatoly, where a meeting between Reagan and Soviet leader Mikhail Gorbachev was set to take place. But the police stopped the rally that Moshe had organized with his young supporters. Moshe was arrested and spent a day in jail. It even made headlines with the national media in Canada. His lawyer was the well-known human rights advocate Irwin Cotler, who a decade later would become a Member of Parliament and eventually Minister of Justice in Prime Minister Paul Martin's government.

Moshe also arranged my final meeting with my old friend from the *Altalena*, Menachem Begin. It was in 1982 and we were in Israel during Operation Peace for the Galilee. Moshe knew of my past relationship with the prime minister and got excited at the idea of getting the two of us together. I couldn't imagine that Begin would have time for us — he might not even remember me. But Moshe, as chairman of an important Jewish youth organization, would not be denied.

And then we got lucky. Moshe discovered that one of Begin's aides was Yechiel Kadishai, the same man who taught me Hebrew in Italy while I was in training for the *Altalena* expedition. Yechiel was now director-general of the prime minister's office, and when Moshe contacted him, he did remember me and promised he'd do everything he could to make the meeting happen. Still, I wasn't holding my breath. Israel was in the midst of a controversial war in Lebanon, and, in fact, had just had eight of its soldiers captured. The government was working around the clock trying to secure their release. Surely, the prime minister wouldn't have time for an old friend he hadn't seen in decades.

And yet, the day came when I astonishingly found myself in the prime minister's reception room, hugging his director-general, even after such a lengthy passage of time. Next thing I knew, we were being ushered into Prime Minister Begin's private office for a meeting. Incredible.

Our meeting began with Moshe telling Begin about the work he was doing as a student activist. He even brought along a suitcase packed with papers, documents, and photos to impress the PM with the job he was doing! Begin seemed impressed with his zeal and enthusiasm. I then asked my son to leave my former Irgun commander and me alone. As we chatted privately for a few moments, Begin and I remembered our younger days on the *Altalena*. We hugged each other and the tears began to flow. When I expressed my concern about the captured soldiers, Begin replied, "Don't you worry. Everything is going to be all right." Then, my former teacher Yechiel took a picture of Moshe and me next to the prime minister, and with that, we left. Remarkably, a few days later, the soldiers were released from captivity. Begin was good to his word. And it was, as I suspected, the last time I ever saw him.

After completing his law degree, Moshe opened his own law practice, but the issues facing the Jewish people the world over and Israel remained the centre of his interests. In 1992 he and I and several others from Toronto traveled to Auschwitz — my first time back inside the gates of hell since escaping half a century earlier. Steve Paikin describes that trip in this book's introduction. Then, in 1998, Moshe was elected president of the Canadian Jewish Congress, at the time, the most important Jewish advocacy organization in Canada, and his work there led us to another memorable visit to Auschwitz, this time with the prime minister of Canada, Jean Chrétien, the details of which he so ably retells in this book's foreword.

After finishing his three-year term as president of "Congress," Moshe continued his community activities as chairman of the Canada-Israeli Committee and more recently as a vice president of the World Jewish Congress. He is happily married to his wife Dara Nathanson, whom he met at York University, and they have two children. Sari was born in 1990, and was named after her grandmother (Ilana's mother). She studied visual arts at York University and is growing into a really talented painter. One of the main topics of her works is the Holocaust, and I can see how important and deep-felt this part of history is to her. In 1996, Moshe and Dara had a second child, a son. They named him Shye, which in Hebrew means "gift." Shye is now in his first year at the University of British Columbia, and he's smart and athletic. But I have wonderful memories of horsing around with him when he was a little kid, getting down on the floor and playing with his building blocks or a game of dominoes. Sometimes Shye and I went to see the Toronto Maple Leafs play. (Don't get me started on whether I think the Leafs will ever win the Stanley Cup in my lifetime!).

My youngest son Dan also went to York University and then to the University of Windsor where he got a double degree in law and business. He opened his legal practice, which has been very successful.

Like Moshe, he has always been closely involved in Jewish life and activities, but Dan has also gotten himself involved in politics. For instance, he worked as a senior advisor to Liberal cabinet minister Art Eggleton in Jean Chrétien's government. Dan did a great deal of the leg work leading to a free trade agreement between Canada and Israel. It was a big step in developing bilateral relations between the two countries. And it meant a lot to me — it made the ties between my two homes closer and stronger.

Incidentally, Moshe also contributed significantly to helping solidify relations between these two nations. Moshe used to work with Gerry Schwartz, the wildly successful Canadian businessman originally from Winnipeg. Gerry is a billionaire who's the chairman and CEO of Onex Corp., the private equity investment firm and holding company. His equally impressive wife is Heather Reisman, the founder and CEO of Indigo Books and Music. The couple was looking for a unique and meaningful way to do something for Israel and Moshe helped them realize that dream. He introduced them to leading figures in Israel, who helped them open an office, start a foundation in Israel, and hire Prime Minister Benjamin Netanyahu's former chief of staff Aviv Bushinsky to run it. They created the HESEG Foundation (HESEG is Hebrew for "achievement").

This program provides academic scholarships and support to young people from all over the world, who have completed military service in the Israel Defense Forces. One of the interesting characteristics of the army is that it is open to anyone, regardless of the ethnic origin or religious belief. At any given moment, up to five thousand young people from different countries are wearing Israeli military uniforms. It is a great tradition, because it shows how welcoming and friendly the Jewish state is — a very different image from stereotypes people often hold. And it also helps to improve the nation's security by attracting ambitious and brave people from around the world. The only problem here is that those young men and women coming from abroad usually have no relatives or friends in their new country, and they face a lot of difficulties settling in Israel if, after completing their military service, they want to stay there permanently. This is where HESEG comes in, helping to provide them with financial support during their years in school and assists in building their careers.

Our lives haven't been without bumps in the road. Unfortunately, Dan's marriage didn't work as well as he had hoped. It ended in divorce, but he has three wonderful children. I should add that I'm truly grateful for the efforts Dan and his kids make to observe Jewish rituals with Ilana and me, whether

it's something as simple as all of us making *kiddish* together, or
as involved as building a *sukkah* (a temporary hut) every year
during the weeklong holiday of Sukkoth (the festival of taber-
nacles). In fact, Dan tells me he asks his kids to say the Shema
every day. And every Friday night when we're together with
Dan's family, each of the grandkids comes to me after we say
*kiddush* and before the hamotze (blessing on the bread) to say
the Shema to me. It's wonderful.

All my grandchildren respect Jewish traditions, they
observe Shabbat and holidays, show vivid interest in the history of Israel, and Sari and Shye are fluent in Hebrew. All of
that gives me one more reason to believe that the pledge we
three surviving brothers made in 1945 at our reunion — to be
strong in allegiance to our faith, history, and ethnic identity —
wasn't in vain. It continues in our children and grandchildren.
In fact, one of the things that gives me the most *naches* (a
Yiddish word meaning intense pride in one's family's accom-
plishments) is something that has become an annual tradition for thirty years: the Ronens have led Jewish high holiday
services, first at York University and now at the Dani Centre
in Thornhill. You cannot imagine the pride I take at seeing
my son Dan reading from the Torah, or Moshe leading the
services, or my grandson Shye blowing the shofar (the ram's
horn). Many of the prayers we say or the tunes we chant are
the same ones I learned as a child in Dej, and I've taught my
own sons to keep these traditions alive.

This whole thing started when my sons were students at York
University. The idea was to give students who couldn't get home
for high holidays a place to come and experience an intimate,

family-like atmosphere. We've often thought the thing had run its course, but people have insisted that we keep providing these services for Rosh Hashanah and Yom Kippur. So we do, even though now, almost no students show up anymore; most of our congregants are people who've come for more than a quarter century. Those original students are now parents bringing their own children. Time marches on, and much to my delight, the Ronens are still doing High Holiday services!

Unfortunately, both of my older brothers are dead now. Both had successful and long singing careers in the United States. It was actually Shalom who first moved to America. However happy and highly valued as a singer he was in Israel, he was never quite satisfied with his situation. Ironically, cantors are better paid outside Israel than inside it. It's supply and demand — there are just too many good cantors in the Jewish state, which makes competition among them particularly fierce. It not only drives down the salaries they can command, but also diminishes the respect and appreciation for their art. Shuli eventually started sending his résumés overseas, and then landed a wonderful job in Minneapolis where he found everything he had been looking for — admiration, esteem, and prosperity. There was a huge dinner in his honour when he retired after many years of service, and there I could see one more time how much he was valued by the members of his community.

Dudi went to the U.S. shortly after we moved to Toronto. First, he worked in Norwich, Connecticut, and later found a job in Baltimore, Maryland, where he stayed until retirement. He also finally found what he had been trying to achieve for many years

— well-deserved recognition of his talent, and a comfortable living. After retirement, he and Olga then moved to New York to be closer to their daughter Sara who lived in Brooklyn.

There was one more significant episode in my life and my brothers were part of it. It should have happened in 1945, but unfortunately, I spent my thirteenth birthday trying to escape Nazi tyranny. So, when my sixty-fifth birthday approached, and my family asked me what I wanted for a present, I said, "I want what I was denied when I was thirteen. I want to have my bar mitzvah."

It's unusual but not completely unheard of for someone to have a bar mitzvah that late in life. In fact, if I can be a little flippant for a moment here, because I hadn't had a bar mitzvah, I was still "officially" a child, unburdened with any responsibilities. I guess it was finally time to grow up.

So, in my home, surrounded by family and friends, Mordechai Ronen finally had a bar mitzvah.

But the best part of the story was the surprise my daughter-in-law Dara organized. At a Shabbat dinner at Moshe and Dara's home the night before my big day, Dara arranged to have my two brothers and their wives flown in to surprise me. As I walked into their home, lo and behold, they were waiting for me. It was a delightful reunion, all three brothers now senior citizens, and it offered us a chance to look back at our lives and take stock of where we were. We had every right to be proud of ourselves. We had jobs, families, and had overcome the tragedies that had dominated our past. It was a great celebration, filled with tears of joy and lots of hugging.

Do I still think about those horrible days back in eastern Europe in the 1940s? Unfortunately, I do. That is no doubt the curse of every survivor: to relive those moments, mourn those we lost, and continue to try to find answers to questions that we know will never be adequately answered.

Were we victims of an epidemic of collective insanity? Was Nazism a kind of infectious disease that had spread over Germany and half of Europe, and put otherwise normal people into a state of delirium, leading to the murders of millions of innocent people? I still don't know.

Our society today tells us that people who are not in command of their senses cannot be found guilty of murder, that they lack the sanity required to be criminally responsible. Does this get the Nazis off the hook? Were they an insane regime and therefore, not criminally responsible for their actions?

I'm sorry, but I just can't accept this. We have to deal with the fact that the Holocaust was perpetrated with sound mind and cold, calculating efficiency, by smart, rational, and well-educated nations. God tells me I have to be understanding and forgiving. But how can I forgive this? How do I forgive those who killed my parents, my two sisters, Suri's unborn child, my cousins, friends, neighbours, and the millions of others who shared their fate?

After the Holocaust, many Jews lost their faith, and it's understandable. Their belief in a loving God that would protect them had been shattered by the Nazi genocide. How could the God they believed in allow such a thing to happen? For them, there was clearly no God at all.

To those people, I say that it is human beings, not God, who built the gas chambers and crematoria. God created us to be free — free to be as constructive or destructive as we want. I chose the good, and I hope I've inculcated my children with those values as well.

Can I forgive what has been done to us?

In 1952 there was a debate in Israel whether to accept money from Germany as compensation for the extermination of the Jews by the Nazis. I spoke to this in an earlier chapter. I saw it back then as a cynical deal, an exchange of the memory of those murdered and our own suffering for a bag of cash. I suspect the Germans would have interpreted accepting the money as forgiveness. Well, no, I can't accept that.

To this day, I have complicated feelings about Germany. In the summer of 2014, while much of the world marveled at Germany's winning the World Cup of football (soccer, as we call it in North America), I confess I couldn't cheer for Germany. My brother Dudi didn't ever want to hear the word spoken in his presence. I will never be a tourist in Germany. The only time I've been there since the war was for a brief stopover at the airport in Berlin on route to Dej. I just have no desire to set foot in the place.

Lest you think I'm tarring the entire German population with one brush, I'm not. I well remember Germans who helped me in the camps, some with food, and others with a few encouraging words. I will be grateful to them to the end of my days. Without them, I wouldn't have survived. Tragically, there were far too few of them. I remember the last glance I took at my mother and two sisters, as they walked away from my father and me, having been promised a hot shower and a good dinner after their long and exhausting trip in a cattle train. Instead they were led to the gas chamber. I can't forget it, and I can't forgive it either.

I remember begging the guards who took my father to his death to give me anything they could to remember him by — bring me his ashes, anything, I begged. They said it wasn't allowed by the rules. No, I can't forgive it. And I never will.

There is a synagogue near my house in Toronto, just as there was all those many years ago in the city of Dej. I go there sometimes to pray and talk to other members of the community. One day, not long ago, I met an older Jewish man there, older than me by five or six years, whose name was also Mordechai. He didn't look very religious but he prayed with the others, and I could see that he was serious. He had recently buried his wife and had come to the synagogue to pay respect to her memory. Then, after shul, we had lunch together and a little drink and he told me his story.

He was from Poland, and as a kid got swept up in the persecutions against the Jews. His chances of surviving were very slim, but he was smart and lucky and managed to escape imprisonment in the ghetto. Instead, he started wandering around the country looking for a safe place, as if there was a safe place for a Jewish boy back then in Poland. He worked on farms for food and shelter, always in fear of being turned in to the police or to the Nazis. He kept changing homes and towns. He was beaten to a pulp, humiliated in thousands of ways, scared to death, starved and desperate, yet he somehow, miraculously, survived.

He's an old man now, modest and humble. He told me at the end of our conversation that he wouldn't even begin to compare his sufferings and losses to mine. But he also said, "I did suffer enough, Motke, I did suffer enough."

He may never have been shipped off to Auschwitz, but the pain and misery he sustained in those years were far beyond anything human beings deserve.

I'm just another insignificant name on the list of the victims of that catastrophe, but one of the luckiest as well. I am telling this story not because I want to scare you, or make anyone feel sorry for me, or to brag about my suffering or heroism. I just wanted to tell the truth. Maybe as you read this book, you'll consider the lives of those who weren't so lucky, who did lose absolutely everything and never had a chance to recover or rebuild their lost homes and families. This book is more about them, than me.

Canada is a great country where people of so many different ethnicities and religions live in relative peace and harmony next door to each other. Ilana and I live in a quiet neighbourhood with friendly neighbours — it actually reminds me a little of the Dej of my childhood. So after all is said and done, I can say that somehow, I have been able to reconnect the two parts of my life — my past in Dej, which was so sweet and beautiful, and my present here in Canada, where I'm surrounded by dear family and friends. Tragically interrupted once, my life is back to where it should be — in a world of love, kindness, and trust.

That's not to say I don't fear for the world nowadays. When the leader of a country such as Iran publicly claims that Israel must be wiped off the face of the map, isn't he expressing the same feeling of racial and religious hatred that once swept over Germany? When Islamist extremists call for a war against anyone who is of a different belief, and chant for death to apostates, isn't that a call for another genocide? When news comes from Hungary that a prominent politician wants his country to make a list of all Jews there, doesn't it sound like we've been here before?

In 2002 I returned to Dej (now, once again, part of Romania) for the first time since I met my three brothers there at the end of the Second World War. The circumstances around the visit were quite extraordinary. My granddaughter Sari had a particularly keen interest in her family's history and a heart of gold to match. So when it came time for her bat mitzvah, her wish was for her family and her grandparents to go to Dej, to see where I grew up. And so we did it.

I found the town almost the same as it was in 1944, when I left it. The same narrow streets with white pretty houses on both sides, cherry and apple trees surrounding them, the same rapid brook with green gardens, bushes, and trees along it crossing the city in the middle, the sidewalks heated in the scorching afternoon sun, beautiful forests around, quiet and affable people, and the gorgeous synagogue still just a couple steps from the house where my family once lived.

But something was different, not just because decades had passed between those two periods in my life, and not just because of the presence of all kinds of modern technology. What was different was that I had lost trust in this place, and would never regain it. Most people, when they visit the place of their childhood, normally enjoy those moments of walking the old streets, entering one's old house, laughing at the memories awakened by the familiar objects or buildings. I was different.

I wanted to run away from the place, especially when I saw the house where I spent the early years of my life. It still looked like the little paradise I grew up in, but its appearance was deceiving.

Interestingly, only one synagogue survived the destruction of Dej's Jewish community — the one near my home. We were able to go inside the building and found it just as beautiful as it was during my childhood years. Memories started flooding back. I remembered exactly where I sat with my own father all those years ago. Now I was in the same spot, with my own son and grandson — three generations of Ronens. Six decades earlier, I had feared mine would be the last generation of my family; that day was a testament to our survival. I put on my *tallit* and *tefillin* and said two prayers: the Shema, Judaism's seminal prayer which acknowledges God's oneness, and the Kaddish, a prayer for the dead.

Of course, the biggest difference between the synagogue of my childhood and the one I was visiting six decades later was that the *shul* was now empty. There were no services, no prayers said, and no worshippers left to fill it. In that respect, the Nazis had got their way — Dej was officially *judenrein*, free of Jews.

Why the Nazis spared the synagogue while destroying all the others isn't quite clear. It may have been that they wanted to use a big, strong building with plenty of storage space inside for their own practical purposes. I also heard another explanation from some of the locals. The synagogue was located on a busy street with many houses next to it. Any attempt to destroy the building, which was built on a solid foundation by skilled construction workers, would probably require a powerful explosion to tear it down, and that could cause too much trouble for local residents. Who knows? For one reason or another, it escaped demolition and is still there — gorgeous, monumental, and empty.

My wife Ilana, my granddaughter Sari, and her family were all there supporting me, but the tears just wouldn't stop flowing. I told my son Moshe that we just had to leave. We went all that way and yet stayed for only three hours. I just couldn't take more than that.

We also went to Lodz, Poland, to see where Ilana started her life. We took to calling this excursion our "Roots Trip," as we explored the roots of three different parts of our family: mine, my wife's, and my son Moshe's mother-in-law Helen's, whose parents were Polish born. When we walked in public areas, we spoke Hebrew amongst ourselves and with our guide. Instantly, I noticed the glances, which I interpreted as irritated and suspicious. We wanted to visit the two homes where Ilana grew up. Our first stop was actually her second home, an apartment building with a courtyard in the middle. It didn't take long before we felt most unwelcome. Eventually, a young guy came out of the building, got in his car, turned on the engine, and instead of driving off, he started revving the engine very noisily. Others were peeking out of their doorways, leering at us. Our guide told us the locals were probably fearful that we were returning in hopes of reclaiming our property. It was a ridiculous thought. We obviously had no such intentions. But the locals weren't done with us. Suddenly, several employees from a bar next to the apartment building came outside, gave us "the finger," put napkins on the sides of their heads to mimic *payot*, and began dancing around as if to make fun of those Jews. It reminded me of one of the great absurdities of our world: persistent anti-Semitism in places where there are no Jews.

Our next stop was to Ilana's first home, and again, it was not an incident-free visit. We stood looking at it from the street. It was a small building with a grocery store on the first floor. We didn't go inside to see my wife's former apartment and we didn't bother anyone with questions. But when my grandson Shye wanted to buy a popsicle at a convenience store across the road, they wouldn't serve us. They rightly assumed we were Jewish (after all, we had a Chassidic-looking guide with us). I guess just standing on the sidewalk and talking to each other in Hebrew was too much of a disturbance for some. That was enough for us, so we left.

In Lodz, we also visited the Jewish cemetery where Ilana's maternal grandfather is buried (he died early, still a young man, before the Holocaust), and where she wanted to see the memorial stones to her other relatives murdered in Nazi camps. We found no stones. The cemetery had been vandalized and all the stones were gone. Someone probably used them to build a fence, a house, or a shed. Ilana decided not to try to restore the graves. Nobody could promise they wouldn't be vandalized again. Instead we arranged for her relatives' names to be written on a monument to Lodz's Holocaust victims.

Not everything on the trip was this sad, and not everybody was that negative toward us Jews. We visited Hrubieszów, a town of less than twenty thousand people in southeastern Poland, because it was the hometown of my daughter-in-law

Dara's grandmother. We met two old women on the street who said "This town hasn't been the same since the Jews left," and she said it with regret. Apparently, before the war, one of the women worked at a factory owned by a Jewish businessman. She told us that it was a good job, where the workers were treated well, and now she felt upset that Jews didn't live in the city anymore.

On the same street, we were also approached by a male stranger whose face and hands were quite dirty. He asked us whether we were Jewish. My son Moshe confirmed that we were. He asked us whether we would like to visit his home for a cup of tea, because he had something he wanted to give us. Naturally, our antennae went up and we wondered about the man's motives, so we sent our guide to go with the man instead. Soon after, the stranger and the guide returned with two pieces of a battered Torah scroll. Apparently, the man was a construction worker who was tearing down a building and found the Torah pieces hidden in the walls. He hung onto the relics in hopes that someday he could give them to Jews who would appreciate having them. We were quite overwhelmed at the man's generosity and my son Moshe insisted on giving him a reward. The man tried to refuse; he just wanted to do a good deed, but we insisted. It was a wonderful reminder that even in a land filled with pain and ghosts, one was still able to encounter random acts of kindness.

Later, we were actually able to read the Hebrew on the Torah remnants. The passage told the story of when God sent angels in the form of men to visit Abraham, the world's first Jew, to tell him he was about to become a father. Abraham welcomed the angels into his tent and served them. It felt like a nice coincidence, given what we'd experienced with our own Polish stranger that day.

We also met a young rabbi who told us his rather unusual story. When he was a child, he knew nothing about his Jewish roots. After the war, his parents gave up their Jewish identity that had caused them too much pain and decided instead to be just another gentile family so that the children wouldn't suffer. Only when he turned thirteen did his mother and father take him to a synagogue, where they revealed what they had been hiding from him for so long. They didn't push him toward rediscovering his roots, they simply wanted him to know the truth. On his own, the man started searching his past. Later, he went to Israel and lived there for a few years studying Judaism, then returned to Lodz as a rabbi. Now, he was at the centre of a small Jewish community, performing services, teaching the language, helping people in any way possible to be proud of their identity, and not to be scared of the hostility of those who see the Jews as the cause of all evil. But again, he was a rare exception.

The Holocaust changed all of us who lived through those times. None of us emerged from the death camps the same people we were before. Many, understandably, lost their minds. Many blocked out the memories and avoided the questions. Nobody can judge them for doing so.

I remember I talked once to a rabbi in my synagogue who wanted to know what happened to me during the Holocaust. When I finished my story he stayed silent for a while, and then asked: "After all of this, do you still believe in God? How can anyone possibly keep his faith after having gone through hell like that?"

"Well," I said, "I always felt that someone was watching over me. And that is what saved me."

Often when I'm in Israel I go to visit the holy Jewish places. One of the holiest is the Kotel, or Western Wall. It's located in the Old City of Jerusalem, at the foot of the western side of the Temple Mount. It is a remnant of the ancient wall that surrounded the Jewish Temple's courtyard, and hardly anything else is dearer to us and more infused with historical and religious memories than this place and the Temple Mount itself.

I went there with my son Moshe for my grandson Shye's bar mitzvah, and when we approached the entrance to the area, an unusual-looking man caught our attention. He was very old, poorly dressed, greeting everyone entering the place. He welcomed them, asked if they needed assistance or explanations, and acted very much like a professional tour guide. Clearly he wasn't one — his age and appearance suggested that. When he greeted us, I was intrigued and wanted to know why this old usher was here? We started to talk, and he told me his story that brought tears to my eyes, because it was almost the same as my own.

The man was born not far from my hometown, in the same part of Hungary, but about ten years earlier. He went, step by step, through the same places and camps that I had. He was taken to the Bungur Ghetto, transported to Auschwitz where he was promised the same thing as every other new inmate — that his only exit from there was "through that chimney." He had lost his family and never fancied his own chances for survival. But he happened to be among those few who were picked for labour camps. At the moment when he was leaving Auschwitz he made a vow to God that if somehow he survived the war and the camps, he would move to Israel and devote the rest of his life to serving Western Wall visitors. And so he did. He never asks for money for his services, never excuses himself from his mission due to bad weather or sickness. He has always considered the fact that he was alive more than adequate compensation for what he was doing. I shared with him my own story, and we stood there, hugging each other, two old men, crying and reliving old memories.

He was about ninety years old, grey-haired with a dignified, wrinkled face. Three years later, my son Moshe went to the same location and there he was, still welcoming people to the Wall.

I never did promise God that I would do something if I survived. But I do have the same sense of indebtedness and duty. Like the man at the Wall, I have the same feeling of being saved from death by some power beyond my intelligence and comprehension. Maybe this book is an attempt to explain that mystery to myself and at least pay back some part of that debt.

In 2012 I was honoured to receive the Community Heritage Award from the Chabad organization in York Region. One of my friends, Anatoly Rozenberg, suggested I tell my story in a book. It's taken a long time, but I'm finally able to talk about this time of my life. And I'm committed to making sure that the younger generations know that this did happen. It happened to me and millions of others. And the world needs to know.

As this book goes to press, I'm eighty-three years old. I'm a happy man, surrounded by loving family and friends. Every morning, I enjoy waking up and facing another day. I'm alive, and free, and still have a little bit of energy to do something good and useful. I take every minute of life as a bonus. God offers us a choice in the Bible. He says in Deuteronomy: "I have set before you today life and prosperity, and death and adversity." He wants us to choose life. I did the best I could at every turn seven decades ago to choose life. And I'm still doing it every day.

I count my blessings every day. I no longer think of myself as a "survivor." I think of myself as a "victor." I've outlasted the Nazis and prostate cancer, and had angioplasty fourteen years ago as well. Not bad for a kid who should have been dead by his twelfth birthday.

In 2011 both Dan and Moshe went on the "March of the Living," one of the most incredible things you'll ever see. Young Jews from all over the world tour Auschwitz on Yom HaShoah (Holocaust Memorial Day), waving Israeli flags. It is the ultimate manifestation of our victory over Hitler. This was Dan's first time in Poland, and so the brothers decided after the event to take a side trip to visit Dej, so that he too could see my hometown (Dan wasn't on the 2002 trip). The same elderly man, who ten years earlier received us there during Sari's bat mitzvah trip, met the boys and opened the synagogue to them. His name was Mr. Farkas. He also accompanied them to my old house on Kodur Street. This time, they found the house slightly renovated, and painted on the outside. On the first visit, the occupants didn't allow us to go inside the home. They had thought, as many do, that we had come to reclaim the home. This time, however, the current residents (a Seventh Day Adventist couple), were happy to invite Dan and Moshe in, once Mr. Farkas explained what their connection to the home was. And then my sons called me in Toronto from inside the house, describing what they saw and answering my questions.

My sons stayed there for a while, and as they were leaving, the owner told them that he made his own slivovitz in the basement. If you don't know, slivovitz is a traditional, strong, vodka-like drink very popular in eastern European countries. He insisted they take back a bottle for me. At first, the boys were reluctant, but he persisted, and they did take it. I'm not much of a drinker, but it was one of the most precious gifts I have ever received in my life. The man who sent it knew exactly what it meant to me. Slivovitz was a standard drink at our Passover dinners. It fills me with appreciation to think of the man who made this meaningful choice for a gift. The slivovitz was made from plums grown on the soil once worked by my father, where once, long ago, I gardened with him, where we all were together, my dad and mom, my sisters and brothers. It tasted sweet and bitter. My childhood, my first memories, my lost home, my pains, and disappointments were all in that bottle. So were my hopes for a better future. Maybe it is a vain hope, but all of that was in my head when I drank a toast with that slivovitz.

In fact, I knew exactly what toast I had to make with this drink when my boys brought it to me. *L'chaim!* (To Life!) I exclaimed as we drank. What other toast could you expect from one of the few who was spared to live? What other toast could there be? "To life!" we all said, as we downed our slivovitz.

To life, indeed.

# Epilogue

## by Steve Paikin

What compels someone to return to the site of one of the most monstrous evils the world has ever known? What provokes someone to walk, once again, under that gate that offered the promise of freedom, if only you worked hard enough — *Arbeit Macht Frei* — but which actually led to an inferno built specifically to obliterate your family, your friends, and your neighbours?

These are questions Mordechai Ronen had to confront in 1992 and 1999 as he travelled to Poland and returned to Auschwitz. Why, yet again, confront the horrors of your past? Why subject yourself to stirring up the painful memories of seeing your mother and sisters led off to the showers and their deaths?

In that fall of 2014, Mordechai faced those questions head on one last time. The government of Poland had decided to sponsor what would likely be the last ever gathering of

Auschwitz survivors, on the grounds of that former killing factory. The occasion was the seventieth anniversary of the liberation of Auschwitz, which would take place on January 27, 2015. No one had confirmed this would be the last opportunity for survivors to gather at the notorious site of so much agony, but given that the vast majority of survivors were now in their eighties and nineties, it seemed likely that it would be. Ten years earlier, at the sixtieth anniversary ceremony, more than a thousand survivors attended. This time, organizers were expecting a fifth of that number to show up. Over the ensuing decade, many survivors had either died or had become too frail to attend the seventieth anniversary ceremonies.

What it meant, of course, is that Mordechai had a decision to make. Should he confront the horrors of his past yet again, at age eighty-two, or be satisfied that his two previous trips to Auschwitz were enough?

As you've no doubt concluded by now, Mordechai Ronen is an extraordinary man. Ever since his return to Auschwitz in 1992, he's been a man on a mission. He's determined to remind the world that the Holocaust did happen, that he was an eyewitness to it, and that he would endure the pain required to admonish the world never to let such tragedies happen again. And so, when the World Jewish Congress and the University of Southern California Shoah Foundation put together a mission for Auschwitz survivors and their families to attend the seventieth anniversary liberation ceremonies — and let Mordechai know that he would be invited to participate — the Ronen family had a decision to make. Organizers offered each survivor the right to be accompanied by an officially

Mordechai's childhood synagogue, the Great Synagogue of Dej. (Photo by Dara Ronen.)

Mordechai and son Moshe pray together at the Great Synagogue of Dej, July 2002. (Photo by Dara Ronen.)

Mordechai stands in front of his childhood home on Kodor Street in Dej, Romania, July 2002. (Photo by Dara Ronen.)

Mordechai's grandson, Shye, stands in the Bungur Forest, the site of the Dej Ghetto, July 2002. (Photo by Dara Ronen.)

Mordechai's siblings and their wives celebrate his sixty-fifth birthday and bar mitzvah, June 1997. From left to right: Shalom Markovits, Dudi Rozencweig, Pnina Markovits, Olga Rozencweig, Ilana Ronen, Mordechai Ronen. (Photo by Dara Ronen.)

Mordechai and wife Ilana celebrate Chanukah with son Moshe, daughter-in-law Dara, and their children, Sari and Shye, December 2011. (Photo by Tobi Liederman.)

Dan and his children. From left to right: Lielle, Ariel, Oriel, March 2012. (Photo by Sari Ronen.)

Mordechai and sons Moshe and Dan lead High Holiday services, September 2014. (Photo by Sari Ronen.)

Mordechai and family stand beneath the famous Auschwitz I gate, January 2015. From left to right: son, Moshe; wife, Ilana; Mordechai; granddaughter, Sari. (Photo by Steve Paikin.)

Mordechai Ronen is once again overcome by emotion at the entrance to Auschwitz I, January 2015. Trying to comfort him are granddaughter Sari, son Moshe, and wife Ilana. World Jewish Congress President Ronald S. Lauder looks on from behind. (Photo by Steve Paikin.)

designated "companion." Sari, as the oldest grandchild and someone who had taken a keen interest in her family's history, told her grandfather she would be prepared to fulfill the "companion" role. And that's how Mordechai decided to return to that place, along with his wife Ilana, his son Moshe, and his granddaughter Sari. (In addition, I was humbled and honoured that the Ronen family wanted me to accompany them on the trip as well. Besides the value of my being an eyewitness to the family's experience for the purposes of this book, Moshe pointed out that it was my questioning of Mordechai on the way to Auschwitz nearly twenty-three years earlier that opened the floodgates, and propelled Mordechai into sharing his history with his family as never before.)

Like many people, Mordechai has an ability to compartmentalize his emotions. So I've learned not to be surprised when, for example, I greeted him at Lester B. Pearson Airport in Mississauga just outside Toronto on January 24, and found him to be in a thoroughly chipper mood. This was the Mordechai who was sort of excited to be travelling overseas with his wife, son, and granddaughter. He likes their company, and the notion of spending a few days travelling with them actually, at that moment, seemed quite pleasant. We flew first from Toronto to Frankfurt, Germany. Our flight left more than an hour late, meaning we'd have to hustle in Frankfurt to switch terminals, find our new gate, then board our connecting flight to Krakow. That kind of tense, long distance travelling can take the energy out of the best of us, but Mordechai and Ilana seemed indifferent to it all. They schlepped their carry-on baggage without complaint through the airport, keeping up a good pace as we arrived at the connecting flight gate just in the nick of time.

Again, arrival in Poland was similarly unemotional. We disembarked from the plane to a bus, then the bus to the terminal, and then stood around for half an hour while waiting for another bus to take us to the hotel. Moshe was sitting on *shpilkes* (a Yiddish expression meaning he had "ants in his pants" or was somewhat agitated) as he tried to connect with organizers, then find transport to the hotel. His parents seemed perfectly calm, in spite of what they knew lay ahead.

The next day, the Ronens picked up where they left off. Despite knowing this day would feature a visit to the gates of Auschwitz and an all too keen understanding of what that would entail, Mordechai was his usual upbeat self over breakfast. He'd tell a joke, or tease Moshe about what he was eating. He didn't betray a single hint of the pain that would emerge later that day. Even during a seventy-five minute bus trip to Auschwitz, Mordechai's compartmentalization continued.

And then we arrived in the town of Oswiecim, near the confluence of the Vistula and Sola Rivers. Suddenly, Mordechai got very quiet. The smile disappeared. The compartment containing his wartime memories was about to open up in a most profound way.

We entered what is now (in Polish) called the Auschwitz-Birkenau Muzeum. Because the attending survivors were special guests of the World Jewish Congress, we were able to bypass the lineup for the metal detector, and in we walked. There is about a five-minute walk from that area to the notorious Auschwitz gate, and throughout the course of that walk, one could see Mordechai begin to tense up. Suddenly, this man who was marching swiftly through airports began to walk slowly, at one point, even limping, taking the arm of his wife or granddaughter for support. His face was transformed. He began to cry.

Mordechai was one of about fifteen Auschwitz survivors to gather at the *Arbeit Macht Frei* gates. Waiting for him and the other survivors at the gates was Ronald S. Lauder, head of the World Jewish Congress. "Welcome," Lauder said to him. Mordechai reached out and hugged him.

The tears continued. There were perhaps twice as many journalists here as survivors, and I saw in them something I've almost never seen in more than three decades of covering public events: I saw respect. I saw tenderness. I saw cameramen and reporters who are accustomed to banging into each other and shouting out their questions to "get the story" showing these survivors a kind of deference they normally never demonstrate. The media were actually showing a reverence for the surroundings that was appropriate. You might not think that's worth noting. But in this day and age, it's an incredible rarity.

"What are you thinking as you stand here," a reporter gently asked Mordechai.

"Horrible place," Mordechai replied, as Lauder puts an arm around him. "Things happened here that we can never let happen again."

Ron Lauder's presence here may surprise some who only know him as a billionaire, one-time candidate for Mayor of New York (he lost the 1989 Republican primary to Rudolph Giuliani), and son of Estee Lauder, the cosmetics legend.

In fact, Lauder has some serious foreign policy chops, having been deputy assistant secretary of defense for European and NATO affairs (1983–86) and America's ambassador to Austria (1986–87). But he may be making his most significant mark on the world as president, since 2007, of the World Jewish Congress, the so-called "diplomatic arm of the world's Jewish community." Lauder has made an unabashed campaign against anti-Semitism one of the hallmarks of his presidency, and to that end, has put millions of dollars of his own personal fortune into the preservation of Auschwitz.

Much of the death camp — the crematoriums and barracks — was destroyed by the Nazis as the war turned against them, and they increasingly wanted to cover their evil tracks. Efforts have been undertaken to reconstruct Auschwitz as it existed in the 1940s, and transform it into a museum, to teach the world what can happen when hate is allowed to flourish unchallenged. But Lauder and others fear the march of time is eroding Auschwitz's rebuilt infrastructure, and so he has invested his own capital into ensuring that the museum is maintained.

That day, Lauder found himself working in another capacity: lending a supportive arm and ear to Mordechai Ronen, who had once again returned to the place where his mother and two sisters were murdered.

"*Abba ... Ima ...* " Mordechai cried out, using the Hebrew words for "father" and "mother." Camera crews from all over the world recorded his every word. The rat-a-tat-tat from the shutters of still cameras was unceasing. Sari held his arm, trying to give him strength, rubbing his back, in effect, performing her role as "companion" and trying to keep Mordechai as calm as possible. Mordechai told the reporters his son Moshe, who's named after his father, was with him.

"I'll tell it to the world," he continued. "I hope it'll never happen again!" Back amidst the barracks and wire fences, he dabbed his eyes with a tissue. There were other survivors there. But Mordechai was centre stage. The cameras almost all focused on him as he continued his monologue. He was not so much talking to any one reporter as he was holding court for everyone within earshot.

"I'm here, and I can tell the world what happened," he said. "I went through this." Then, referring to his wife, son, and granddaughter, he said: "They give me the courage to be here. I wanted to be here because I can tell what happened. To all the people denying it, you can see me here. And I can tell you, it happened."

Sari continued to stay close to her grandfather. She too looked overcome by the intense emotion, but didn't allow that to deflect her from her role, which was to assist her grandfather on his journey. Moshe and his mother Ilana also watched Mordechai carefully. They were torn. On the one hand, they supported his decision to return and fully appreciated Mordechai's mission, given that Moshe himself spent decades travelling the globe, fighting anti-Semitism and working to support Israel. But they were both deeply concerned about the pattern these trips can manifest. Mordechai can quickly become deeply morose, descending into an increasingly agitated state, so much so, that it becomes nearly impossible to stop the tears from flowing. Moshe has learned that the key is to find just the right moment before stepping in, interrupting his father's monologue, and stopping it all. It's hard to know when. He knows Mordechai needs to get the deeply pent up emotions out of his system. It's cathartic. And it's part of the mission. But he also knows his father can tumble into an agony where he appears to be on the verge of a nervous collapse.

"I'm strong," Mordechai yelled through his tears, crying with increasing volatility. "I'm a victor! I lived!"

Moshe and Ilana watched carefully. They sensed that the moment where they would need to intercede was close at hand. Mordechai continued, now talking one-on-one to CTV National News reporter Ben O'Hara-Byrne, and getting increasingly agitated.

"They were murdered here," Mordechai said of his family members. "I'm here to tell the world. It was difficult but I had to do it. I hope this will be my last time to say goodbye to my parents. My father, my mother, my two sisters...." Mordechai sobbed, on the verge of a meltdown. "I couldn't even say goodbye...." Ilana leaned over to Moshe saying, "It's enough, I think he's had enough."

"Come," Moshe said to his dad, interrupting the soliloquy, putting his arm around his tormented father, and bringing the interview to an end. Mordechai cried, but the rest of his family's influence calmed him down.

One still photographer had an idea. He wanted all fifteen survivors to pose for a picture with Ron Lauder under the *Arbeit Macht Frei* sign. It took some doing, getting all the survivors under the sign, and getting everyone else out of the way. But eventually, it happened. By then, Mordechai had stopped crying and had a stoic look on his face. One female survivor even shouted out: "We should all return in ten years!"

"I agree," said Lauder. But unsaid, yet understood, was that this was almost certainly the last time many — if not all — of these survivors would gather here.

The photo taken, Sari held her grandfather's arm. With all of the survivors gathered around him, Mordechai decided to lead the group in saying the Kaddish, the Hebrew prayer for the dead. Again, he started calmly, but before long became increasingly agitated. By the time the prayer came to an end, Mordechai again invoked the names of his murdered family members.

"*Abba, Ima*, Tobi, Sarah," he shouted, overcome with tears. "Never happen again! I don't want to come here anymore!"

Again, Moshe recognized his cue. He began to sing "Hatikvah," Israel's national anthem. Everyone else picked up the tune. It served its purpose; Mordechai instantly pulled himself together and joined in the chorus. When the anthem ended, Mordechai again took the lead, reciting the Shema, the ancient Jewish prayer recognizing God's oneness, that Jews have often recited throughout history before death and prior to being murdered.

With that, the group of survivors disbanded, but the morning's events were not over. The survivors continued to give interviews and Mordechai continued to answer questions. I could not imagine that Mordechai had an ounce of emotion left. He had by then spilled so much of his guts. But the reporters had more questions. And Mordechai obliged them. He simply wanted to do everything possible to get the story out. And his companion Sari was right by his side, holding his hand, lending support.

"My mother and two sisters went to the left," he told a BBC reporter. "I went with my father to the right. That's why I survived. I was with him for seven months in labour camps. He died and I had to take him out." Mordechai began to cry again. "I asked if I could have his ashes, but they said no. From that time on, I started to live. I said I WILL SURVIVE!" Mordechai was again in full rhetorical flight. "All I could think was, I want to live," he continued. "And I survived."

He related what other prisoners had told him upon his arrival at the camp.

"'You see the flames there? You're going to be burned alive.' But I was selected to live. I'm a survivor, but I'm a victor. The more I saw, the stronger I got. Every day I got stronger."

Mordechai started to cry again. So his granddaughter picked up the story. "My grandfather focused on building his family back up," she said. "I've been lucky to have him and he's shared stories with me." Mordechai kissed her as she finished.

It was then time to go. And once again, I saw something I had never seen before. Members of the media began to hug the survivors. There was a collective recognition that this was not just another story to get on to the news that night. This was different. The journalists had been genuinely affected by what they had seen and heard.

Mordechai and the rest of his family began to depart. "This is my last time here," he said to no one in particular. He was utterly spent. We all piled into a van waiting to take us back to Krakow. It was a quiet ride back to the city; not much conversation in the van. It had been all too much to process.

We arrived back in Krakow and a news crew from CBC-TV's *The National*, sent over from Toronto, awaited us in the city's central square. They hadn't come to Auschwitz that morning but still wanted Mordechai and Moshe's views on what transpired, and the state of anti-Semitism in the world today. Before the interview, Moredechai, Ilana, Moshe, and Sari did some "walking shots" for the camera. Reporter Havard Gould would record a voice-over for his report for the news the next night. It had been an awful day for Mordechai but, inspired by his mission, he answered producer Carla Turner's questions.

"How does it feel to be back here in Poland?" she asked.

"I was obliged to come," Mordechai began. "I felt it my duty to be here and to tell the story of what I went through when I was in Auschwitz. To educate young people to know what happened. This was my main purpose to be here. It was very hard and very emotional for me."

This interview not only took place the day before the seventieth anniversary of Auschwitz's liberation. It also happened a little more than two weeks after terrorists in France massacred the staff at the *Charlie Hebdo* magazine office and attacked a kosher market in Paris as well. In light of all of that, Moshe was asked about what he'd now like to see take place.

"We hope leaders will take action to obliterate hate and intolerance and anti-Semitism," he began. "The freedom to hate, the freedom to kill and murder, we have to combat that through legislation and speaking out against the hate and anti-Semitism and intolerance that is so widespread today."

Two other things are worth noting about this interview. At the interview's conclusion, the producer, Carla Turner, reached out and touched Mordechai's arm. Again, that's something you just don't often see in the daily grind of journalism.

The other thing I noticed wasn't quite so touching. As the Ronens were doing their interview, a man who looked to be in his fifties walked behind them and clearly muttered "Zydo," the Polish equivalent for the slur "kike," while the CBC crew was taping its interview. It was a sobering reminder that there is still much work to do.

Of course, the main reason for the Ronens' trip to Poland was yet to come. January 26 was a gruelling day for the family, but it was a small, almost private experience compared to what lay ahead on January 27, the day of the actual seventieth anniversary liberation ceremony. Once again, the Ronens would bus to Auschwitz, but this time, they would be accompanied by three thousand spectators, not to mention high-ranking dignitaries from forty countries.

The following day, Mordechai and his family made their way back to Auschwitz. More than seventy years ago, he and his family were stuffed like cattle into a railway car and shipped off to Auschwitz, as the world chose to look away. But on this day — January 27, 2015 — he and his fellow survivors received a police escort to the same location to stand with world leaders in a show of solidarity. And the procession wasn't just a few police cars leading a convoy of buses. The Polish government surely recognized what a disaster it would have been to have a terrorist incident at this event, so it looked as if scores of security vehicles had blocked every side street that intersected with the main roadway leading to Auschwitz to secure the event.

The buses took us to a different location in the Auschwitz complex, a few kilometres away at Birkenau, where the trains arrived during the war. Because of the frail state of so many survivors, organizers decided against an outdoor service and instead erected a massive tent attached to the world's most notorious watchtower, where Josef Mengele, with the flick of his wrist, selected men, women, and children for life or death. We arrived a good ninety minutes before the ceremony would take place. It gave all of us a chance to wander around and inspect the surroundings. The organizers had built a clear, Plexiglas cover on top of the train tracks that took more than a million people to their deaths. Attendees could and did walk on top of the glass. We also had time for some informal conversations with others before the official program began.

The CBC News Network had called earlier asking Sari if she would do an interview from the site. She had done a few interviews with Mordechai in Toronto before leaving for Poland, and was willing to do another, inside the actual death gate watchtower in Birkenau. Despite dealing with her own sense of being overwhelmed at this location, she did an excellent job being interviewed "live" by the CBC's Heather Hiscox.

As Sari was interviewed, I began wandering through the tent, looking for others to talk to. I was also determined, through Twitter and Facebook, to share whatever stories I could about the people I was encountering. It has not been a frequent occurrence in my journalistic life to be in a place which actually could be considered the most important story in the world on that day. But on January 27, I was convinced we were all in the most newsworthy, important place in the world.

I happened upon another group of survivors from Toronto. One man was wearing a name badge which said "Martin Baranek." That rang a bell. I approached him.

"You're Martin Baranek?" I asked him. He said yes. I said, "You're not going to believe this, but I was in your corner store on Keele Street in Toronto when David Peterson announced he wanted to put beer and wine into corner stores in that 1985 provincial election campaign. That was almost thirty years ago!"

Baranek's reaction was fabulous. "It wasn't a corner store," he corrected me. "It was a supermarket!" We then reminisced about that campaign, which saw Peterson eventually become premier of Ontario. And we both had to shake our heads in amazement that here, twenty metres from one of the most horrendous places on earth, we found ourselves talking about Ontario politics. Baranek was thirteen years old when sent to Auschwitz. He survived there for six months, and endured thirty-one months in total in several concentration camps.

The encounters became increasingly compelling. I met Alex Speiser, who was part of a group of two thousand young boys from eastern Europe who were transported here. Only he and two others survived.

I met Angela Polgar who was born in Auschwitz on December 21, 1944. Her mother Vera was two months pregnant upon arrival in Auschwitz. Somehow, she survived Mengele's experiments and secretly delivered Angela in a barrack. But she immediately had to hide her baby as only two hours later she had to appear at a roll call outside in bare feet, in the middle of winter. Fortunately, Auschwitz was liberated five weeks later. Both mother and daughter survived the war, and Vera actually lived into her seventies. Angela's father didn't. She never met him, as he died in Auschwitz. This was Angela's first trip back to the death camp since liberation day seventy years earlier. She brought along her daughter Katy. Angela is thought to be one of just two people alive in the world today who were born in Auschwitz.

As the few dozen international leaders began to take their seats to the left of the stage, there was another well-known figure taking his seat off to the right. He was surrounded by officials and the scene certainly conveyed a sense of "do not approach." But Moshe Ronen has never been one to be easily deterred. And so he waded his way through a group of officials and approached the man who was now seated.

"My father is a survivor of Auschwitz," he told the man. "I'm sure you get asked this all the time, but I'm sure he'd be thrilled to meet you." The man leaped to his feet and said he would be honoured to meet Moshe's father.

And that's how Mordechai Ronen met Steven Spielberg, the man who, in nearby Krakow, made the film *Schindler's List*, the Academy Award winner for best picture in 1993, and who created the USC Shoah Foundation, which has archived 53,000 interviews of Holocaust survivors as a permanent record of testimony.

The night before this ceremony, Spielberg gave a speech at a Krakow hotel, at which many of the survivors were present. "We're once again facing the perennial demons of intolerance," Spielberg told the audience. "The most effective way we can combat this intolerance and honour those who survived and those who perished is to call on each other to do what the survivors have already done: to remember and to never forget."

Spielberg, of course, is responsible for some of the biggest box office hits of all time including *E.T. The Extra-Terrestrial*, the Indiana Jones series, the Jurassic Park films, *Saving Private Ryan*, and *Jaws*. But he confessed that, until he made *Schindler's List* and created the USC Shoah Foundation, he never truly felt in touch with his Jewish roots.

"I'm grateful to these survivors," Spielberg continued, "not only for their bravery in the face of genocide, but because in wanting to help them find their voices, I got to find my own voice, and I got to find my own Jewish identity."

Now, a day later, Spielberg found himself in an impromptu conversation with one of those survivors.

"I'm honoured to meet you," Mordechai said to Spielberg.

"No," Spielberg replied, "I'm honoured to meet you." For the next couple of minutes or more, the two chatted as if they were long-time friends — the small businessman from the north end of Toronto and the filmmaker whose motion pictures have grossed billions of dollars.

"Thank you for what you have done," Mordechai said, wrapping up their conversation as the program was about to begin. Again, Spielberg pushed back. "No," the filmmaker insisted. "I thank you for what you have done."

What a moment.

Even Spielberg's personal assistant, who witnessed the encounter with tears in her eyes, told Sari that her boss meets so many people, but she had never seen him react in such a personal and meaningful way to an encounter with a survivor. She and Sari shared a brief cry.

Attendees were urged to take their seats and the first speaker was the event's "patron," Polish President Bronislaw Komorowski, the only politician who would speak at the event. "The Nazis made Poland a cemetery of Jews," the president said. "Our duty is to remember for those who suffered."

Then, one after another, several Holocaust survivors took to the stage to say their piece. Halina Birenbaum was the first.

"This was a bottomless pit of hell I could not get out of," she said, referring to her time in Auschwitz. "But I lived to see those oppressors defeated. I lived to see the defeat of those henchmen."

Roman Kent, an eighty-nine-year-old survivor, was frequently interrupted by applause because of his grandiloquence. "How long was I here?" he asked rhetorically. "I don't know. One minute was like a day. One hour was like a year. One day was like a lifetime."

Kent enthralled the audience with lines such as, "Hate is never a right; love is never wrong," and "We do not want our past to be our children's future. This is the key to my existence."

He chastised the media for their use of inexact language, for example, when reports suggested more than a million people were "lost" in Auschwitz. "These people weren't lost," Kent insisted. "They were murdered. Not to describe it as it was diminishes our outrage and protects the perpetrators."

And then, most significantly, Kent put the horrors of Auschwitz into a modern context. He told his audience, "If you will remember this and reach others, then Darfur, Biafra, Serbia, and the attacks in Paris will have no place in our world." He concluded, "We should add an eleventh commandment — you should never be a bystander."

Once again, Ilana sprang into action. The survivors and their spouses were sitting in a special section near the front of the tent. By this point, Mordechai had again dissolved into desperate emotional state. Ilana walked towards the back of the tent where Moshe and Sari were sitting.

"He's crying all the time," Ilana told her son with sympathy. "He needs your help." Moshe switched seats with his mother, and tended to his distraught father.

The program next featured a documentary made by Spielberg especially for this ceremony. It was a stark recitation of the facts, narrated by the brilliant actress Meryl Streep, explaining how the most efficient killing machine in world history came to be. The documentary was brief but incredibly powerful. At its conclusion, the audience applauded its approval of Spielberg's efforts to bring the lessons of the Holocaust to the world. As Spielberg's image appeared on the many television screens placed around the setting, we could then see a short man with a yarmulke on his head approaching the world-renowned filmmaker. He shook Spielberg's hand, congratulating him on a job well done. It was Mordechai Ronen.

The final speaker of the day was Ronald Lauder, who was born less than a year before Auschwitz's liberation. With forty world leaders, including the presidents of Germany, France, Italy, and Poland, sitting only metres away from him, Lauder didn't pull his punches. He acknowledged it was the Nazis who perpetrated the evil we had gathered to remember, but that almost every other country in Europe was complicit. He expressed his outrage that it was 2015, but for too many Jews, the re-emergence of so much anti-Semitism made them feel as if it were 1933 all over again.

"Your governments must stand up to this new wave of hatred," Lauder growled, staring directly at the world leaders to his left. "There must be zero tolerance of hatred of any kind. The world's silence and indifference leads to Auschwitz. Do not let this happen again!" It was powerful stuff, and we've reprinted most of this excellent speech as an appendix to this book.

Over the next half hour or so, those international dignitaries that Lauder admonished left the tent, marched outside in the cold to the Gate of Death to light a candle and place it at the gate's monument. Upon their return to the tent, again, there was another unusual moment. At the conclusion of the service, rather than being whisked away by their security details, the world leaders stuck around and waded into the crowd. Most impressive was France's President François Hollande, who on at least three occasions rebuffed staff members who were trying to get him to leave. Hollande must have spoken for a half an hour with Holocaust survivors. His message was a clear rejection of Israeli Prime Minister Benjamin Netanyahu urging that Jews leave France and come to Israel. Hollande wanted these survivors and the world to know that, despite the increasing anti-Semitism in France and the recent terrorist attacks, that France is still home to its Jewish inhabitants. As Hollande's prime minister, Manuel Valls, had said earlier in an impressive speech: "France without Jews would not be France."

Other politicians including Italian President Pietro Grasso, German President Joachim Gauck, and Ukrainian President Petro Poroshenko also mingled with survivors. Canada's three main federal parties were represented by Multiculturalism Minister Tim Uppal, New Democratic Party MP Pat Martin, and Liberal MP Marc Garneau. At a news conference at the Holiday Inn Hotel in Krakow that morning, Martin confessed he'd never been to Auschwitz before, "But I've been told to brace myself." For his part, Uppal, the first turban-wearing Sikh cabinet minister in Canadian history, had proposed the creation of a government-sponsored Holocaust monument in Canada, as his first private members' bill. The bill passed unanimously in 2011 after Uppal noted Canada was the only allied nation without such a monument. His wife Kiran is also thought to be the first non-Jew ever to walk in the "March of the Living," (a two-week trip to Poland and Israel, traditionally taken by Jewish teenagers) something she did long before her husband was in politics.

Four hours after we had arrived at Birkenau, it was time to leave. As we exited the massive tent, my arm around Mordechai's shoulder, I said to him: "Mordechai, you won. Hitler lost. You've told the world. And now you never have to come back here again."

As we walked outside into the snow towards the buses waiting to return us to Krakow, I sensed Mordechai Ronen finally had some peace. He will never totally be at peace — that would be impossible. But perhaps he has achieved some. Sari said her grandfather later told her that the trip had rein-vigorated him — given him a new sense of purpose — that will add ten years to his life.

The next day, we all took a taxi to the Krakow Airport to head home to Toronto. Our driver was a Polish man, probably in his forties, who mostly listened to our conversation as we drove the half-hour to the airport. Halfway there, in heavily-accented English, he summoned up the courage to interject a question into our conversation. Taking his gaze off the road for just a second, he turned around to look at Mordechai.

"Are you a survivor of the Holocaust?" he asked.

"Yes I am," Mordechai answered.

The driver paused for what seemed an eternity before speaking again. Finally, he did.

"Very big respect," was all he said.

The University of Toronto's Holocaust scholar Michael Marrus once wrote that Holocaust history is like all history in this respect: it must constantly be rewritten, so as not to lose its significance. And since the public is constantly dealing with new interests, it's incumbent on each successive generation to retell the stories to their unfamiliar fellow citizens.

Mordechai Ronen returned to Poland on this terrible anniversary and put himself through the emotional turmoil of telling his story to ensure two things: first, that the world knows the Holocaust happened, and second, that it must never happen again.

He accomplished the first part of that mission.

However, as Michael Marrus suggested, the second part of that mission never ends.

# Acknowledgements

## from Mordechai Ronen

For nearly fifty years, I couldn't talk about my connection to the Holocaust. I just couldn't. Even today, when I talk about it, I'm quickly reduced to tears. It's an agony that just doesn't go away.

But clearly, I've made progress. It started in April 1992 while on a bus ride to Auschwitz — my first return to that concentration camp since I'd been there as a child. My friend Steve Paikin was on that bus ride and through his questions, I began to talk about my personal experiences for the first time. It was a bit of a breakthrough. Another friend and Holocaust survivor, Nate Leipciger, was also on that bus, and as he talked about his experiences, my "opening up" continued. Nate returned to Poland numerous times and used his experience to educate many. So let me begin this acknowledgements chapter by thanking them.

But the person who really convinced me to share my story in a book is my good friend Tony (Tevia) Rozenberg. Tony urged me to put my experiences on paper, thinking it would be cathartic for me, and both useful and important for those who read this. Thank you Tony for giving me the boost I needed to get this done. Like your late parents Nela and Simon, you have continued to be wonderful friends. (Author's note: Tony says Mordechai "has every right to be bitter and angry with the world. But instead, he's the most normal, modest, decent human being around. He's my hero.")

I also need to thank former Prime Minister Jean Chrétien, not only for providing the foreword for this book, but also for inviting me to go back to Auschwitz with him. His support during that visit was instrumental in my getting through it.

Kirk Howard, the president and publisher of Dundurn Press, readily admitted he hadn't published much before in this genre, but he was receptive to taking on this project. So we thank him and his staff, in particular Michael Melgaard, who was our main contact and copy editor.

While concentration camps in Poland were a death factory for too many Jews, I do need to acknowledge that there were two non-Jewish Poles without whose help I wouldn't have survived. They were my fellow prisoners — political prisoners in their case — and their first names were Mietek and Staszek. I have no idea of their whereabouts today. They're probably dead. But without them, I have no doubt I wouldn't have survived the war.

Three other friends read the first draft of the manuscript and made excellent suggestions on how to improve it. Danny Eisen, a long-time family friend, has been a community activist with my son Moshe since their student days. Gerard Walsh is a childhood friend of my daughter-in-law Dara's. He's a historian and teacher in St. John's, Newfoundland. And Jonathan Kessler spends his days as Leadership Development Director for the American Israel Public Affairs Committee. He's also a friend of Moshe's, read the manuscript, and made some excellent suggestions to bring the larger themes of the book into sharper view. Thanks to the three of you for making this book better than it otherwise would have been.

Kudos as well to Nick Zyuzev, who also played a part in getting this project started. Nick did some initial research at Tony Rozenberg's request, and put together a rough draft that was helpful in the early stages. Marc Nadeau pitched in with his editing skills on those early drafts. It all made a contribution to this finished product.

I also need to thank my family, whose love and patience have sustained me all these years. No one could ask for a more loving wife than my Ilana. My sons Moshe and Dan, about whom I've already written, have been stalwarts. It cannot have been easy having a father who wears the burden of his past on his sleeve as I do. But I'm so proud to have them share my name. And I should add Moshe's wife Dara to the list. She's been like a daughter to me.

Of course, the great joys of my life are my five grandchildren, who continue to give my life meaning. I do need to single out the oldest — Sari — because of the wonderful contribution she made to this book. Sari worked closely with Steve, did independent research and fact-checking, gathered pictures and anecdotes from me, explored my family's background and family tree and did so much to make this book happen. Sari has even taken to speaking to high school classes about the

Holocaust. Education is the key to ensuring tragedies like this never happen again, and I'm so proud that she's doing her part on that front. I'm also very proud of Ronald S. Lauder, president of the World Jewish Congress, and all the work is he doing to promote Holocaust education. His presence at my trip to Auschwitz earlier this year was incredibly meaningful.

And finally, I need to thank God. In spite of it all, I still believe in God. I still believe his looking out for me enabled me to survive the Holocaust. For that, I shall always be grateful, as long as I have breath left in me.

# Appendix 1:

## "Do Not Let This Happen Again," a speech by Ronald S. Lauder

On January 27, 2015, three thousand people gathered at the gates of hell.

The Polish government mounted a moving ceremony to mark the seventieth anniversary of the liberation of the Auschwitz-Birkenau concentration camp. About two hundred survivors of that camp attended, along with their families, companions, and dignitaries from more than forty countries worldwide.

Of the many superb speeches given that that event was one from Ronald S. Lauder, president of the World Jewish Congress. He did not sugar-coat his remarks, and in fact, stared directly at the international leaders as he uttered his final line, which is the title of this chapter.

Here are excerpts from that speech:

I am not a survivor, although I am grateful for the survivors who are here today. I am not a liberator, although I salute the courage of the veterans who are among us today.

I am here, simply, as a Jew. And, like all Jews everywhere, this place, this terrible place called Auschwitz, touches our souls.

I have always wondered if I had been born in Hungary, where my grandparents were from, instead of New York in February of 1944, would I have lived?

The answer is no. I would have been one of the 438,000 Hungarian Jews gassed by the Nazis here in Auschwitz in 1944.

What was the reason that over one million Jews were murdered right here? The reason was they were Jewish. Nazi Germany believed Jews had no right to live. Yes, the Holocaust was designed by the Nazis. But there was complicity from almost every country in Europe.

I was going to make a very different speech here today. But after the recent events in Paris, throughout Europe, and around the world I cannot ignore what is happening today.

Jews are targeted in Europe once again because they are Jews. Synagogues and Jewish businesses are attacked. There are mass demonstrations with thousands of people shouting death threats to the state of Israel and to Jews.

Shortly after the end of World War II, after we saw the reality of Auschwitz and the other death camps, no normal person wanted to be associated with the anti-Semitism of the Nazis.

For a time, we thought that the hatred of Jews had finally been eradicated. But slowly the demonization of Jews started to come back. First in articles and on the Internet, in some religious schools, and even universities. From there it made its way into mainstream society.

It happened so slowly and it all seemed so unimportant that few people paid any attention.

Until now, when Europe suddenly awoke to find itself surrounded by anti-Semitism again and it looks more like 1933 than 2015.

Once again, young Jewish boys are afraid to wear yarmulkes on the streets of Paris and Budapest and London. Once again, Jewish businesses are targeted. And once again, Jewish families are fleeing Europe.

How did this happen? Why, after seven decades and three generations, is this new storm of anti-Semitism sweeping through Europe and targeting Jews?

For decades, the world has been fed lies about Israel: that Israel is the cause of everyone's problems, that Israelis are the villains of the twenty-first century, that Israel has no right to exist.

We all learned that when you tell a lie three times and there is no response, then the lie becomes the truth.

This vilification of Israel, the only Jewish state on earth, quickly became an opportunity to attack Jews. Much of this came from the Middle East, but it has found fertile ground throughout the world.

The targets of this hate are not just Jews. Christians are being slaughtered in Africa and Syria. Women and girls are killed in Afghanistan just for wanting to go to school. Journalists are murdered in the Middle East and right here in Europe a terrible wave of hatred has descended on our earth once again.

There are representatives from forty nations here with us today and we, the Jewish people, are so grateful that you have joined us. You are good, decent people. But because of where we are and what this place means your governments must stand up to this new wave of hatred.

Schools must teach tolerance of all people. Houses of worship should be places of love, understanding, and healing they should not be telling their people to kill in the name of god. All countries and the European Union must make hate a crime. Any country that openly brags about the annihilation of another country should be excluded from the family of nations. Every government must have absolutely zero tolerance for hate of any kind.

Unless this is checked right now, it will be too late. We still have a chance to stop this, but if every government does not act quickly, then the tragedy of this terrible place will darken our world again.

World silence led to Auschwitz.

World indifference led to Auschwitz.

World anti-Semitism led to Auschwitz.

Do not let this happen again.

# Appendix 2:

## Ronen Family Tree

1. Moshe Markovits, my father, born in 1899 in Satu Mare, Romania; murdered in late 1944 in the Gusen death camp, near Linz, Austria.
2. Elka Markovits (nee Harnik), my mother, born in 1900 in Năsăud, Romania (family originally from Vienna, Austria); murdered May 1944 in the Auschwitz II-Birkenau death camp, Oswiecim, Poland.
3. Tova "Tobi" Markovits, my sister, born in 1920 in Dej (Dés), Romania; murdered in May 1944 in the Auschwitz II-Birkenau death camp, Oswiecim, Poland.
4. David "Dudi" Rozencweig (born David Markovits), my brother, born May 17, 1922 in Dej, Romania; died March 31, 2000 in Brooklyn, New York.
5. Shalom "Shuli" Markovits, my brother, born January 10, 1924 in Dej (Dés), Romania; died November 12, 2012 in Minneapolis, Minnesota.

6. Sara "Suri" Markovits, my sister, born in 1929 in Dej (Dés), Romania; murdered in May 1944 in the Auschwitz II-Birkenau death camp, Oswiecim, Poland.

7. Mordechai "Motke" Ronen (born Mordechai Shlomo Markovits), myself, born June 5, 1932 in Dej (Dés), Romania. Lives in Toronto, Ontario.

8. Olga Rozencweig (nee Solomon), my sister-in-law, wife of David, born November 14, 1924 in Újfehértó, Hungary; lives in Brooklyn, New York.

9. Sara Weingarten (nee Rozencweig), my niece, daughter of David and Olga, born April 24, 1947 in Milan, Italy; lives in Brooklyn, New York.

10. Pnina Markovits (born Rubina Haim), my sister-in-law, wife of Shalom, born August 15, 1932 in Corfu, Greece; died April 24, 2013 in Minneapolis, Minnesota.

11. Ilana Ronen (born Liliana Perlberg), my wife, born October 25, 1937 in Lodz, Poland; lives in Toronto, Ontario.

12. Leon "Lolek" Perlberg, my father-in-law, born January 1, 1911 in Wloclawek, Poland; died June 8, 2004 in Ramat Gan, Israel.

13. Sara Perlberg (nee Konvale-Katz), my mother-in-law, born May 18, 1913 in Lodz, Poland; died January 26, 1990 in Ramat Gan, Israel.

14. Moshe Ronen, my son, born December 6, 1958 in Ramat Gan, Israel; lives in Toronto, Ontario.

15. Dan Ronen, my son, born March 9, 1964 in Ramat Gan, Israel; lives in Toronto, Ontario.

16. Dara Lyn Ronen (née Nathanson), my daughter-in-law, wife of Moshe, born August 25, 1959 in St. John's, Newfoundland; lives in Toronto, Ontario.

17. Sari Cyma Ronen, my granddaughter, daughter of Moshe and Dara, born May 7, 1990 in Toronto, Ontario; lives in Toronto, Ontario.

18. Shye Rafael Ronen, my grandson, son of Moshe and Dara, born February 13, 1996 in Toronto, Ontario; lives in Toronto, Ontario.

19. Lielle Yaffa Ronen, my granddaughter, daughter of Dan, born January 4, 2003 in Toronto, Ontario; lives in Toronto, Ontario.

20. Ariel David Ronen, my grandson, son of Dan, born March 30, 2006 in Toronto, Ontario; lives in Toronto, Ontario.

21. Oriel Nissan Ronen, my grandson, son of Dan, born March 30, 2006 in Toronto, Ontario; lives in Toronto, Ontario.

# Yiddish and Hebrew Glossary

Yiddish is a language that's been around for more than a thousand years. Its roots are in ninth-century central Europe. The words sound German but are written with the Hebrew alphabet. It was the main language of my youth, and as a result, there are many Yiddish terms sprinkled throughout this book. I thought it might be helpful to present a list of those Yiddish and Hebrew words here.

bimah: the podium or stage at the front of the synagogue.

chayder: an after-school program of Jewish studies.

kapos (a German word): prisoners in concentration camps given special duties and responsibilities by the German officers.

| | |
|---|---|
| kinde: | child. |
| mensch: | a decent, honourable human being, who acts with integrity. |
| meshuggah: | crazy. |
| naches: | intense pride in one's family's accomplishments. |
| payos (in Hebrew, payot): | the ringlets of hair on each side of the head, traditionally worn by ultra-Orthodox Jewish men. |
| schluf: | sleep. |
| sheitel: | a woman's wig. |
| shul: | synagogue. |
| tallis (in Hebrew, tallit): | prayer shawl. |
| tateh: | father. |
| tefillin: | phylacteries — two small, black leather boxes that are worn on the head and arm, containing verses from the Torah. |
| tzitzis (in Hebrew, tzitzit): | the four-cornered ritual garment with a series of strings and knots on each corner. |
| upsherin: | a young Orthodox Jewish boy's first haircut. |
| yeshivas: | Jewish seminaries. |